British India: The History and Legacy of the British Raj and the Partition of India and Pakistan into Separate Nations

By Charles River Editors

"Troops of the Native Allies", a contemporary lithograph

About Charles River Editors

Introduction

A depiction of Sepoy officers in the 1820s

British India

"A significant fact which stands out is that those parts of India which have been longest under British rule are the poorest today. Indeed some kind of chart might be drawn up to indicate the close connection between length of British rule and progressive growth of poverty." - Jawaharlal Nehru, *The Discovery of India*

The British East India Company served as one of the key players in the formation of the British

Empire. From its origins as a trading company struggling to keep up with its superior Dutch, Portuguese, and Spanish competitors to its tenure as the ruling authority of the Indian subcontinent to its eventual hubristic downfall, the East India Company serves as a lens through which to explore the much larger economic and social forces that shaped the formation of a global British Empire. As a private company that became a non-state global power in its own right, the East India Company also serves as a cautionary tale all too relevant to the modern world's current political and economic situation.

On its most basic level, the East India Company played an essential part in the development of long-distance trade between Britain and Asia. The trade in textiles, ceramics, tea, and other goods brought a huge influx of capital into the British economy. This not only fueled the Industrial Revolution, but also created a demand for luxury items amongst the middle classes. The economic growth provided by the East India Company was one factor in Britain's ascendancy from a middling regional power to the most powerful nation on the planet. The profits generated by the East India Company also created incentive for other European powers to follow its lead, which led to three centuries of competition for colonies around the world. This process went well beyond Asia to affect most of the planet, including Africa and the Middle East.

Beyond its obvious influence in areas like trade and commerce, the East India Company also served as a point of cultural contact between Western Europeans, South Asians, and East Asians. Quintessentially British practices such as tea drinking were made possible by East India Company trade. The products and cultural practices traveling back and forth on East India Company ships from one continent to another also reconfigured the way societies around the globe viewed sexuality, gender, class, and labor. On a much darker level, the East India Company fueled white supremacy and European concepts of Orientalism.

In Bengal, the region where the rebellion that would change British-Indian relations permanently took place, the Company shared power with a local nawab. The Company was given increasing responsibility, including the power to collect taxes, or Diwani,[1] in 1773. Many have criticized this "Dual Authority" of both local Indian rulers and the rule of Company officials as allowing for greater corruption and creating anger and resentment throughout Bengal.[2] Though a defender of Britain's contributions to India's history and economy, Kartar Lalvani calls the Company's collection of the Diwani "short-sighted greed" and charges the Company with a "horrendous blunder concerning the role of revenue collection."[3]

To the Indian people, the events of 1857 are known as the first War for Independence. For the British, the time is referred to as a mutiny, an uprising, or a rebellion.[4] It is ironic that a similar

---

[1] Percival Griffiths, The British Impact on India (London: MacDonald, 1952), 77.
[2] Ibid., 143-7.
[3] Ibid., 10.
[4] John Keay, India: A History. New York: Atlantic Monthly Press, 2000. 437.

story played out just under 100 years earlier, during the American Revolution, or as the Americans called it, the War for Independence.

Whatever the moniker, in 1857, one of the Indian armies, the Bengal, mutinied. [5] In the most cursory histories of the period, the cause of the rebellion is simply cited as an oversight, a change in the type of grease used in powder cartridges rumored to contain animal fat. This revelation horrified both Hindus and Muslims. The British response, which either failed to recognize the need to address the growing rumors or attempted to force Muslim and Hindu soldiers to use the ammunition despite their objections, made things worse. Author John McLeod explains that though the controversy over animal-greased rifle cartridges was the immediate cause of the conflict, economic, religious, and political resentment existed and had been worsening throughout 1856.[6] He also argues that rather than the uprising being attributable to either one incident or one cause - such as concerns over attempts at religious conversion by Christian officers, anger at the British in general, or frustration over specific tax policies - the rebellion was fueled not only by those with specific complaints against the British, but by those who sought to end up on the right sight of history. McLeod argues that many Indians joined the rebellion only after the tide seemed to be turning in favor of Indian rebels: "In general, the deciding factor was whether or not such leaders felt that their interests and those of the people under their command would be best served by ending British rule."[7] McLeod concludes that the basis of the mutiny was ultimately economic, observing that "the commercial and educated classes of Calcutta, Bombay, and Madras had prospered under Company dominance, and held back."[8]

The rebellion was filled with internal conflict and rivalries among various groups, but one would be hard-pressed to find an author who does not cite the uprising of the Bengals as a turning point in British-Indian relations.[9] Though the cartridges greased with animal fat were withdrawn from service almost as quickly as they had appeared, the damage had already been done. The newly issued rifles required these cartridges to be opened with teeth prior to being jammed in the barrel of the rifle.[10] Long-term resentment toward British expectations and demands boiled over since "to cow-reverencing Hindus as to pig-paranoid Muslims the new ammunition could not have been more disgusting had it been smeared with excrement; nor, had it been dipped in hemlock, could it have been more deadly to their religious prospects."[11] Rumors about the British "tricks" spread quickly, as did resentment and mistrust.

An estimated 80,000 Indians and over 5,000 British were killed during the rebellion, often

---

[5] John McLeod, The History of India (Westport, CT: Greenwood Press, 2002), 81.
[6] Ibid.
[7] John McLeod, The History of India (Westport, CT: Greenwood Press, 2002), 82.
[8] Ibid.
[9] John Keay, 437.
[10] Ibid., 438.
[11] Ibid.

horrifically, and as British historian Percival Griffiths said of the rebellion in retrospect, "It is useless to pass judgment on these excesses on both sides. Cruelty begets cruelty, and after a certain stage of suffering and horror justice and judgment give way to the demand for vengeance. All that can be said is that both amongst Indians and English the Mutiny brought out the best and the worst."[12]

Once it had put a stop to the rebellion by defeating the various Indian rebel groups individually,[13] the British government ended up ruling India directly. However, as McLeod pointed out, "Like much of British imperial expansion, taking formal control of India was not intentional. Instead when British lives and trading interests (represented by the East India Company) were threatened by violent reaction to encroaching westernization, London felt obligated to step in to take control of both the situation and the country."[14] The news was delivered to the Indian people in a proclamation by the English government in 1858.[15]

Ultimately, the East India Company's activity across the Indian subcontinent led to further British involvement there, and the British Raj, a period of British dominance and rule over India that formally began in 1857 and lasted until 1947, remains a highly debated topic amongst historians, political scientists, the British people, and the people of modern India. In Martin Deming Lewis's *British in India: Imperialism or Trusteeship*, he attempts to settle the question, opening with opposing views of those closest to British India:

> "No romance can compare with the story of the handful of Englishmen . . . who, beginning as mere traders and merchant settlers, have in barely two centuries built up the majestic structure of an Imperial system under which peace, order and good government are secured for three hundred and fifty millions of human beings inhabiting what is in essence a continent of its own." - A 1942 Raj official

> "Those parts of India which have been longest under British rule are the poorest today. . . Nearly all our major problems today have grown up during British rule and as a direct result of British policy: the princes; the minority problem; various vested interests, foreign and Indian; the lack of industry and the neglect of agriculture; the extreme backwardness in the social services; and, above all, the tragic poverty of the people." -Jawaharal Nehru, imprisoned Indian reformer, 1944

How can it be that two contemporaries view the same phenomenon so differently? Without a full understanding of the Raj, simplifications and hastily-drawn conclusions are the only possible

---

[13] John McLeod, 83.

[14] Robert Carr, "Concession & Repression: British Rule in India 1857-1919: Robert Carr Assesses the Nature of British Rule in India during a Key, Transitional Phase," *History Review*, no. 52 (2005).

[15] Sneh Mahajan, British Foreign Policy, 1874-1914: The Role of India (London: Routledge, 2002), 37.

outcomes. Instead, it's necessary to seek an understanding of the people, forces, and events shaping the history of British India to arrive at valid conclusions about the British-Indian experience and to understand the continued divide over its legacy. Perhaps then it's possible to answer Lewis's question: "Is it possible that British rule was both destructive and creative at the same time?"[16]

British India ultimately covered some 54 percent of the landmass and 77 percent of the population. By the time the British began to contemplate a withdrawal from India, 565 princely states were officially recognized, in addition to thousands of zamindaris and jagirs, which were in effect feudal estates. The stature of each Princely State was defined by the number of guns fired in salute upon a ceremonial occasion honoring one or other of the princes. These ranged from nine-gun to twenty-one-gun salutes and, in a great many cases, no salute at all.

The Princely States were reasonably evenly spread between ancient Muslim and Hindu dynasties, but bearing in mind the minority status of Muslims in India, Muslims were disproportionately represented. This tended to grant Muslims an equally disproportionate share of what power was devolved to local leaderships, and it positioned powerful Muslim leaders to exert a similarly unequal influence on British policy.

It stands to reason, therefore, as India began the countdown to independence after World War II, that the Indian Muslim leadership would begin to express anxiety over the prospect of universal suffrage and majority rule. At less than 20 percent of the population, Indian Muslims would inevitably find themselves overwhelmed by the Hindu majority, and as the British prepared to divest themselves of India, ancient enmities between Hindu and Muslim, long papered over by the secular and remote government of Britain, began once again to surface.

British India: The History and Legacy of the British Raj and the Partition of India and Pakistan into Separate Nations looks at the centuries of British involvement in the region and its aftermath. Along with pictures and a bibliography, you will learn about British India like never before.

---

[16] Martin Deming Lewis, ed., British in India: Imperialism or Trusteeship? (Boston: D.C. Heath, 1962), vii.

The Dominance of the British East India Company

Sir Charles Wood (1800–1885) was President of the Board of Control of the East India Company from 1852 to 1855; he shaped British education policy in India, and was Secretary of State for India 1859–66.

Europeans had been seeking Asian spices, silks, and other goods since at least the Middle Ages. Prior to the early modern period, most of these products had to be transported along the Silk Road connecting China to South Asia and Europe. While trade between these regions existed, it was at a smaller scale compared to the trade within and between the major Asian empires. This was largely due to the relatively poor nature of European goods; European civilizations simply did not produce anything of comparable value to Asian goods. In addition, transporting goods across land meant that each commodity changed hands several times between

East Asia and its eventual European consumer; as a result, only the wealthiest members of European society could afford to purchase items like silk and pepper (Blaut, *Colonizer's Model*).

This imbalance in commodities and resources changed with the European colonization of North and South America. In South America, the Spanish found enormous quantities of silver in the Bolivian mines of Potosi. The silver bullion and other mineral wealth harvested from the conquest of the New World finally gave European nations a trading commodity that appealed to merchants and rulers in Asia. The introduction of Bolivian silver into the global economy followed quickly on the heels of expeditions such as Vasco da Gama's rounding of the Cape of Good Hope, which allowed for travel to Asia by sea instead of by land. These two factors together provided the catalyst for renewed European interest in Asian trade (See Stein, *Silver, Trade, and War*, 52). Despite increased mobility and access to resources, long-distance trade between Europe and Asia remained extremely dangerous and expensive in the 17th and 18th centuries. As it was rarely feasible for an individual merchant or small merchant company to undertake the journey, a new form of organization emerged, the joint stock company.

The British East India Company was founded in 1600 by several London merchants through a Royal Charter from Queen Elizabeth I. The Dutch East India Company (VOC), which formed almost simultaneously, quickly had considerable successes bringing goods from Asia to Europe, while the Spanish had by far the greatest foothold in the New World and the Portuguese had been at the forefront of African and Asian exploration. Essentially, the East India Company emerged at a moment when the British appeared to be at a disadvantage compared to their European rivals.

It is also important to note that despite its later significance in the formation of the British Empire, the East India Company did not initially form with colonialist motives. At its start, it focused strictly on trade by means of establishing outposts in overseas ports, forming trading partnerships with local merchants, and cornering the market on profitable goods in particular regions (Marshall, "British in Asia," 490-91). The East India Company formed during a period when similar ventures were being formed for other parts of the world; trading companies sought profits in British North America, the Pacific, and South America. While other ventures initially had more success, the East India Company eventually became the most profitable and influential.

In the 1600s, India was open to a number of foreign traders and had agreements, not only with the British but also the Dutch, the French, and the Portuguese. In fact, it was partially in the interest of Indian leaders, such as Mughal emperor Jahangir[17], to invite the British into a closer relationship with India to counter the influences of the proselytizing Catholic Portuguese.

Although it was technically a private company rather than an organ of the British state, in some ways Britain's East India Company operated like its own country, including engaging in such practices as diplomacy and having its own armed forces. In other ways, however, it was very

---

[17] Ian St. John, The Making of the Raj: India under the East India Company (Santa Barbara, CA: Praeger, 2012), 3.

much a business enterprise, the central concern of which was profit. These two functions and their goals were sometimes directly opposed to each other; maximizing profits could lead to starvation and rebellion, while effective governance sometimes meant taking less profitable measures. This tension was constantly at work not only in India but in the interactions between the British Crown, the Court of Directors who dictated major decisions in India, and the people on the ground there.

The British East India Company sought a number of Indian products for export to the homeland or other British colonial destinations, including cloth, silk, indigo, saltpeter, and spices like pepper and cardamom."[18] Thus, at the beginning, "the relationship between Indians and Britons was a purely commercial one. The impact of the British on the cultural life of India was marginal and neither side could have anticipated that this handful of traders would come to dominate the subcontinent."[19]

It was, according to many traditional British historians, the decline of India that led to her initial subjugation. Percival Spear, professor and author of multiple works on Indian history, asserted that when the officers of the British East India Company began arriving in India, they "found a country in ruins…Not only did they encounter dismantled fortresses and deserted palaces, but canals run dry, tanks or reservoirs broken, roads neglected, towns in decay, and whole regions depopulated…India was exhausted and for the moment without inspiration… Everywhere the links between the rulers and the people had been snapped…The rule of force was universal and politically there was no hope."[20]

Many modern writers and commentators, however, rail against the idea that India was in need of British aid, or that India was even in a state of decline to begin with, calling these claims "inadequate and self-serving."[21] Instead, they argue the British historically disguised their imperial designs on the country as necessary and humanitarian interventions. Ian St. John, though an apologist for this view, cautions against a simplistic interpretation of the British role in the eventual subjugation of India. The Raj, he claims, "that ultimately emerged was neither planned nor envisaged at the commencement of the process. Any suggestion that the East India Company would come to occupy the imperial throne vacated by the Great Mughal would have appeared outlandish to Britons and Indians alike."[22]

St. John also argues that it is important to understand that the Raj, rather than something that happened to Indians, was a phenomenon brought on by the operation and even design of particular Indian sub-groups; that "Important sections of Indian society have as fair claim to be considered the architects of the Raj as the British themselves."[23]

---

[18] Ibid., 11.
[19] Ibid., 4.
[20] Ibid., 8.
[21] Ibid.
[22] Ibid., 10.

Moreover, for the first hundred years of its existence, the East India Company could hardly be considered a resounding success. It quickly landed in India and signed its first treaty with the Mughal Dynasty in 1615, securing the right to trade from a factory in Surat (Timeline). From there, they traded in textiles, indigo, cotton, and saltpeter, the last of which would eventually become one of the most important commodities to come out of India due to its use in gunpowder. However, this was at the time considered a minor achievement. At this point, the East India Company's Court of Directors had its sights on Southeast Asia rather than India, seeking to gain a foothold in places like Sumatra in order to compete against the Dutch spice trade there. These efforts were small in scale and not very profitable. A few outposts, known as factories, were established in Sumatra and other islands in the Indonesian archipelago, but these were closed down by the Dutch. Japan and China both stood out as highly desirable trading partners, but Europeans had little success there in the 17th century; Japan's Tokugawa Shogunate closed the country to all foreign traders except a handful of Dutch merchants, while China allowed foreign trade under highly controlled circumstances. In short, the major Asian empires still controlled most of the trading activities in the region. Even among European powers, the East India Company lagged behind the VOC and the Spanish Crown, which controlled the Philippines (Marshall, 490-91).

The East India Company's fortunes began to change in the early 18th century. Around 1700, East India Company merchants redirected their attention to India and established factories in several major cities, most notably Calcutta. These factories produced immense quantities of textiles and spices. In the 1720s, the profits of the East India Company finally exceeded those of the VOC as the British began to pull ahead of their European competitors in Asia. From this point on, the economy of Britain, its North American colonies, and Western Europe as a whole became heavily intertwined with Indian trade (Marshall, 490-91).

In the 1700s, India was ruled by a number of princes kept in power by mercenary forces. It was the norm then, and not the exception, for the British East India Company, which had growing interests to protect in Madras, Calcutta, and Bombay, to employ Indian soldiers for their cause. Unlike many other proprietors, the Company had a reputation of paying on time and without fail. As an attractive employer, the British East India Company would eventually come to dominate large parts of India, not with Anglo armies–which amounted to only 10% of the Company force–but with Indians: "It was, in other words, an Indian army that conquered India for the British."[24]

This is not to say all relations between Indians and the Company were friendly. It must be remembered that in the mid-1700s, the British were not building an unchallenged empire as many modern historians paint it, but actually competing with rivals for economic dominance. The British had built Ft. William in Calcutta as a defense against the rival French East India

---

[23] Ibid.
[24] Ibid., 12.

Company.

The East India Company's approach to India also changed dramatically in the 1740s. Where East India Company merchants had once been content with small outposts and factories in Mughal-controlled territories, where they had once thought more of profit than of territory, they began to act more as agents of imperial expansion. The reasons behind this shift are complex, but one major factor was the outbreak of the Seven Years' War. The Seven Years' War, considered by some historians to be the first truly global conflict, featured warfare between Austria and Prussia in Europe and their allies, and the French and the British in the colonial theaters. The war reached the Indian Ocean in 1744 when naval battles erupted between the French and the British. Two years later, war broke out between two Indian rulers: the Nawab (a term roughly equivalent to governor or provincial ruler) of Arcot, a British ally, and the Nizam of Hyderabad, a French ally. Operating largely as a proxy war between the two European powers, the conflict had a severe and negative impact on the local population.

At the war's end, the Nawab of Arcot stood victorious but saw his status reduced to that of a client state of the East India Company (Marshall, 492). Thus, the East India Company began to assert itself as a major figure in Indian politics and conflicts between different regional authorities. These changes coincided with similar changes in approach in the Dutch and French empires, with the new imperial turn in India coinciding with colonial efforts in Indonesia and the Pacific. Since many of the East India Company's choices abroad were driven by competition with other European states, it comes as no surprise that all of the major European powers adopted similar tactics.

In 1756, war broke out again, this time between the East India Company and the Nawab of Bengal. During the course of the fighting, 146 prisoners were locked, at the nawab's orders, in an 18 by 14-foot cell inside the fort, resulting in the death of nearly 50. The reports of the infamous "Black Hole of Calcutta" in lurid detail by British writers, created an anti-Indian fervor throughout Britain and affirmed the superiority of Anglo rule as necessary for the civilization of the country in the British mind.[25]

---

[25] Richard Cavendish, "The Black Hole of Calcutta." *History Today* Volume 56. Issue 6. June 2006.

A contemporary depiction of the Nawab of Bengal

Depictions of soldiers at the battle

As trade within India increased in volume and value, the stakes for political control grew greater. The British, still reeling from the events of 1756, believed it necessary for their own defense (physical and economic) to have Company-friendly rulers on the thrones in areas of trade, and the Company involved itself in an Indian political dispute in Bengal to ensure such an outcome. It was, as St. John reminds his readers, not the "conquest of Bengal as such. The extension of British power occurred via the East India Company and proceeded in piece-meal fashion over several years. Even then it was not initiated with this end in view, followed no preconceived plan, and was certainly not endorsed by politically-conscious opinion within Britain. What…drove events forward were the actions of a few "private enterprise imperialists" motivated by the prospect of monetary gain. These men, also, possessed no plan and were drawn into the vortex of Bengali politics by sectional interest groups who wished to utilize the military services of the Company in their own power struggles…"[26]

Rather than a planned "conquest," the British operated on a "principle"—"it was permissible to use force to reconfigure the internal politics of Bengal if this appeared the path of greatest net benefit to the Company. The interests, rights, and attitudes of Indians themselves were an irrelevance."[27]

While historians typically mark the Battle of Plassey in 1757 as the true starting point of British rule in India, resistance continued in various forms. Peasant revolts and uprisings, while never successful in driving out the East India Company and their local representatives, occurred with regularity. In 1783, a massive peasant uprising in Rangpur took control of entire regions for over a month, going so far as to elect their own government and replace the old ruler with a new Nawab. East India Company officials brutally suppressed the uprising, which had consisted of men and women from a large cross-section of Rangpur society. At the direction of the East India Company, soldiers put down the revolt by killing civilians without trial. Subsequent peasant revolts erupted throughout the early 19th century. Most of these revolts began as a response to the economic strain of production quotas and tax collection. While some succeeded in inflicting violence and destruction on the East India Company and its local representatives, peasants were never able to form a coalition with which to engage in sustained fighting (Sen, History Modern India, 84-85). Riots and rebellions would erupt, swiftly overtake a region, and then burn out or face opposition once they reached the neighboring province.

Elites continued to engage in more organized military resistance. The most notable of the post-Battle of Plassey figures to challenge East India Company rule was heir to the kingdom of Mysore, Tipu Sultan, who engaged in a series of four wars against East India Company incursions into his kingdom, conflicts collectively known as the Anglo-Mysore Wars. Tipu

---

[26] Ian St. John, 19.
[27] Ibid., 19-20.

Sultan was notable for his extensive efforts to assemble an international coalition to oppose British influence in South Asia but despite his best efforts, he was killed in battle in 1799. This is generally considered the last serious attempt to check British expansion across the Indian subcontinent (Roy, War, Culture, and Society, 87).

A depiction of Tipu Sultan

A painting depicting the death of Tipu Sultan at the Battle of Seringapatam in 1799

What's In a Name?

In 1808, Charles Stuart, an English soldier and lover of Indian culture, questioned conventional wisdom, primarily the need for India to be "civilized" by her British conquerors. He asked, "What is wisdom? And what is civilization? Had not the Hindoos[28] brought the arts of peace to their highest perfection; and recalled in astronomic science, the philosophers of Europe; ere the lust of conquest in the eleventh century had impelled to their shores, the hostile hordes of the west? And under the subsequent dominion of those invaders, was it not ultimately found necessary to govern them with due attention to their own laws, manners, customs, and religion?"[29]

Nonetheless, the prevailing view among the British was indeed the opposite for centuries, despite the sentiments of Stuart, and those of William Dalrymple, the best-known author of British-Indian history, who noted that "India has always had a strange way with her conquerors.

---

[28] Throughout this work, British spellings of Indian names have been kept intact, reflecting the British control of the country during the period. When appropriate, or to avoid confusion when quoting authors, Indian spellings and/or names are substituted and noted.

[29] Charles Stuart, *Vindication of the Hindoos from the Aspersions of the Reverend Claudius Buchanan, M.A.* (London: R and J Rodwell, 1808). 119-120.

In defeat, she beckons them in, then slowly seduces, assimilates and transforms them." Until a stunning turn of events in the mid-1850s, Britain, from her perspective, sought to improve, exploit, educate, and civilize the Indian continent through the auspices of the British East Company, a corporation whose fortunes and territories had grown until two-thirds of India was in their control by 1857.

However, that year an event which changed not only British and Indian, but world history took place. Over 800,000 Indians and thousands of Britons were killed, a once-great trading company was destroyed, and a great transfer of power from the company to the hands of the British government was exchanged. An event of this significance must have a name, as naming is a way of communicating about a fixed period. Names are imbued with meaning. Tellingly, the naming of the 1857 event has taken on a deliberative, if not oppositional nature, partially due to arguments about its scope, partially to the views of the historians who chronicle it.

In the *Journal of Political Studies*, author Syed Hussain Shaheed Soherwordi points out four names that have been used to describe what happened in 1857: "mutiny, uprising, war of independence, and revolution."[30] He discounts the name Sepoy Mutiny because of its "trivial connotations depicting the incident as an act of treason by a group of soldiers," rather than as a wider and more long-term rebellion against British rule. He argued that by calling the incident a mutiny, Britain was attempting to maintain the falsehood that the large majority of Indians supported the British presence and that only a limited number of unhappy Sepoy Hindus were, in fact, rebelling against her.[31]

Because of their limited geographic scope, and the division amongst Indians themselves as to support of the British during the conflict, Soherwordi also rejects the terms War of Independence or revolt as fitting names for 1857.[32] Soherwordi argues that the most appropriate term is indeed uprising, since the rebels cause was not united, but rather based on the desires and motivations of individuals and local bands. Biswamoy Pati, a professor of history at the University of Delhi, also eschews the name "Sepoy Mutiny," writing instead of the "Great Indian Rebellion of 1857."[33] Regardless, what the British called the Sepoy Mutiny or Sepoy Rebellion would change both countries permanently.

The Origins of the Rebellion

In October of 1857, the *London Quarterly Review* published a previously released article on the Sepoy Rebellion in standalone form. At the top of the article, a note of explanation appears: "No. XVII of the London Quarterly Review having been speedily sold off, and considerable

---

[30] Syed Hussain Shaheed Soherwordi, "The Significance of the Different Names Applied by Historians to the Events of 1857," *Journal of Political Studies* 20, no. 1 (2013).

[31] Ibid.

[32] Ibid.

[33] Biswamoy Pati, *The Great Rebellion of 1857 in India.* (New York: Routledge, 2010).

inquiry for the following article still existing, it is issued in a separate form."[34]

The topic of the much in demand commentary was ammunition, or rather, the grease purportedly used on cartridges that had been disseminated to Sepoy troops in India. Whether rumor, reality, or blunder, some sepoys had come to believe the grease used on the cartridge wrappings was made of animal fat. The authors, having provided a quick geography and history of India and her religions and castes, bemoaned the "enormity of the blunder" of the greased cartridges that had set off an Indian rebellion as "almost incredible inattention to the habits of the people" and "an affront exactly prepared to frighten and wound both Hindu and Mussulman alike. A Brahmin will shriek with terror if a drop of pure water from a glass in the hand of a European fall upon him by accident; and how any Government, having even heard of India, not to say knowing it, could allow the issue of the greased cartridges to such men, is one of those marvels of human folly, in presence of which it is impossible to be angry, it looks so like judicial blindness."[35]

The *Quarterly* argued that the main mistake of the British in the years leading up to 1857 had been her abandonment of the "outcastes," those who had been defiled and were thus relegated to the outskirts of Indian society. As the *Quarterly* claimed, somewhere between 1 in 5 and 1 in 10 Indians living outside of India's social, economic, religious, and political life, which provided an opportunity for the British to tap into this class of disaffected people and build an army of support who saw an opportunity for redemption in merit, not by birth or circumstance. Instead, the authors charged, the British had been attracted by the lure of the "Brahmins and Musslemans" who insisted that the only pure people were those who abided by their strict dietary and associative rules. The British, in the desire to build the most respectable of armies, had traded the loyalty of the outcastes for the approval of the Hindu and Muslim elites. The result, the *Quarterly* argues, was an army that considered caste preservation as far more important that any loyalty to the British crown.[36]

Defending England against the charges that more recent cultural policies had caused the rebellion, the *Quarterly* pointed to the English influence on the right of widows to remarry, the rights of Indians who had converted to Christianity, and on missionary education and other efforts of Christian missionaries.[37] While freely admitting "that the sermon, the book, the school, are surely and irresistibly working their way into the heart of the nation," the authors argued that the missionary efforts have been the most well-received and popular of all of Britain's endeavors in India, pointing out the full-to-capacity schools and the lack of any incident of complaint or conflict between the missionaries and the people.[38]

---

[34] "The Sepoy Rebellion". *The London Quarterly Review*. No. XVII, October 1857, ii.
[35] "The Sepoy Rebellion", 14.
[3636] Ibid., 16-21.
[37] Ibid., 20-27.
[38] Ibid., 27.

Returning to the earlier discussion of the greased cartridges, the *Quarterly* claimed that "had the question of the greased cartridges been submitted to a jury of Missionaries, they would, to a man, have decided against any such attack upon the prejudices of the people; for they know what does and what does not irritate…What they feared was 'not conversion, but contamination.'"[39]

The Cambridge Shorter History of India takes nearly the opposite view, claiming that whatever the true intentions of the British government, the actions of Christian missionaries and educators had convinced the Indian people that their entire cultural system, including the caste system, was about to change: "Such notions, false as they were, spread alarm, anxiety and distrust through large masses of the population," claimed the editors.[40]

Additionally, Britain's multiple conflicts, including her losses to Russia in Afghanistan, damaged the empire's credibility abroad —including in India, and bitterness of specific people groups over new British policies that appeared to lessen their importance or privilege add fuel to the fire. In fact, according to the authors, "in 1857 India was afflicted by a considerable number of causes all making for unrest and uncertainty: schools and mission houses, the maintenance or disgrace of undesired widows, family bitterness over conversions followed by an enforced partition of the family property, Muslim discontent, the Oudh talukdars' bitterness -- none of these by itself of great moment, none likely to produce more than a sporadic movement, but collectively making up a situation full of alarming possibilities."[41]

The Earl of Dalhousie, who ruled India as Governor-General from 1848-1856, fervently believed in the goodness of British rule and wanted to see its benefits extended to as many Indians as possible. His reforms included the restoration of inheritance rights to converts from Hinduism, the right of Hindu widows to remarry, and the continued creation of a modern infrastructure that would bring India into modern times.[42] Therefore, "public works of undoubted utility, like surveys, roads, railways, telegraph lines, and irrigation schemes, were bringing government into direct contact with the rural masses and dramatically demonstrating its power as an agency for change. On the new maps, it looked as if India was about to be ensnared in a steel tangle of wires and railway tracks."[43]

---

[39] Ibid., 27-28.

[40] J. Allan, T. Wolseley Haig, and H. H. Dodwell, *The Cambridge Shorter History of India*, ed. H. H. Dodwell (Cambridge, England: Cambridge University Press, 1934), 729.

[41] Ibid., 732.

[42] John Keay, *India: A History*. (New York: Atlantic Monthly Press, 2000), 432.

[43] Ibid.

James Andrew Broun-Ramsay, The Earl of Dalhousie

In Delhi, to the north of the modernization, sat the man who would be one of the last Mughal Kings: Mirza Fakhour. He was concerned with preserving his extravagant lifestyle, paid for by the British, but also his line, and he was in communication with Dalhousie about which of his sons would be recognized as the next Mughal leader after his death.

It was tradition for Mughal rulers to house a court poet who both entertained and advised the princes through verse and observation. Mirza Fakhour's court poet, Ghalib, was an insistent and jealous man who thought highly of himself, even writing to Queen Victoria to ensure her understanding of his special status in the Mughal's house and therefore to Britain. Ghalib warned his patrons of the great changes taking place: "See the sahibs of England! They have gone far ahead of our Oriental forbears. Wind and wave they have rendered useless. They are sailing their ships after fire and steam…With their magic, words fly through the air like birds. Air has been set in fire…cities are being lighted without oil lamps. This new law makes all other laws obsolete."[44]

Other changes took place in the legal code. The doctrine of the lapse, later one of the most criticized Dalhousie policies, was introduced officially in 1848, though it may have been in practice earlier. The doctrine meant that "if the ruler of a State created by or subordinate to the Company died without natural heirs, his State lapsed to the Company--adopted heirs could only inherit if their adoption had been sanctioned."[45]

Dalhousie's ultimate intentions concerning the doctrine of the lapse remain a matter of debate. Certainly, Dalhousie indicated that the doctrine would allow Britain to be rid of several unjust rulers who used hereditary arrangements with the East India Company to remain in positions of power and extreme wealth, while exploiting, or at best ignoring, the native peoples under their rule. By holding the right to decide whether a prince's descendants had a legitimate right to rule, Dalhousie reasoned, Britain could more justly rule India.

Soon after the Sepoy Mutiny, the doctrine of the lapse was heavily repudiated. During Dalhousie's time as Governor-General, however, the annexations of Indian lands were popular, both for bettering the lives of the Indian people, extending British rule, and for the monies that would be added to the treasury as the economic benefits of new lands flowed into British coffers.

During Dalhousie's time in India, there were six areas subject to the doctrine of the lapse.[46] One of Dalhousie's more controversial takings was the Kingdom of Oudh in 1856. Here, the king was removed from his throne before his death (Oudh's annexation thus went beyond even the doctrine of the lapse) based on his incompetence,[47] as well as his character, which was "excessively debauched."[48] The annexation of Oudh (or, as the Indians called it, Awadh) proved controversial.

Though the British claimed that the removal of Nawab (King) Wajid Ali Shah was necessary for the rights of the Indian people, some later historians have defended him: "Cast by providence for the role of an accomplished dilettante, he found himself a misfit for the high office to which he was elevated by chance. Wajid Ali Shah's character was complex. Though he was a man of

---

[44] William Dalrymple, *The Last Mughal: The Fall of a Dynasty: Delhi, 1857.* (New York: Alfred A. Knopf, 2007), 122-3.
[45] Percival Griffiths, *The British Impact on India* (London: MacDonald, 1952), 100.
[46] Ibid.
[47] Robert Shadle et al., eds., *Historical Dictionary of European Imperialism* (New York: Greenwood Press, 1991), 302.
[48] William Dalrymple, 118.

pleasure, he was neither an unscrupulous knave nor a brainless libertine. He was a lovable and generous gentleman. He was a voluptuary, still he never touched wine, and though sunk in pleasure, he never missed his five daily prayers. It was the literary and artistic attainments of Wajid Ali Shah which distinguished him from his contemporaries."[49]

Wajid Ali Shah

One Thomas Bird, a servant of the East India company, claimed that the criticisms of Oudh as a Kingdom of "crime, havoc, and anarchy by the misrule of a government at once imbecile and corrupt" were "a fiction of official penmanship"… proven false "by one simple and obstinate fact" that the people of Awadh clearly "preferred the slandered regime of the Nawab to the grasping but rose-colored government of the Company."[50] Similarly, a Sepoy perspective on the annexation is found in the account of Sita Ram, who, though remaining ultimately loyal to the British as a soldier, nevertheless was critical of the British policy in Oudh. Interestingly, Sita Ram's account of Indian resentment contains no religious concerns, but focuses on the economic status of sepoys who had come to be landowners in Oudh, as well as political resentment over the apparent disregard for the Indian rulers. He describes how the rumor of the taking "led to

---

[49] G. D. Bhatnagar, *Awadh under Wajid `Ali Shah* ([1st ed.]). Bharatiya Vidya Prakashan, Varanasi, 1968.
[50] William Dalrymple, 118-119.

great excitement within the army which was largely composed of men from Oudh. Many of them did not much care whether the Sirkar (the government) took Oudh or not, but these were men who owned no property there. Nevertheless, an undefined dislike and disquiet took possession of all of us... the Sirkar removed the Nawab to Calcutta and took over the government of the Kingdom. Regiments of local infantry and cavalry were formed officered by English office and a number of Assistant Commissioner sahibs were brought in. Many of these officers came from the Bombay and Madras Armies and were totally ignorant of the language, manners, and customs of the people, and the same was true of all the sahibs who came from Bengal from the colleges. The occupation of the country was effected without any open resistance at the time. It took place so quickly that the people did not have time to combine against it but the minds of all the Taluqdars and headmen were excited against the Sirkar, which in their view had acted dishonorably, and had been unfair to the Nawab. There were plenty of interested people to keep this feeling alive. They assured everyone that the estates of the rich would soon be confiscated by the Sirkar, which could easily manipulate the law courts to show that the present owners had no right to these estates. The truth was that so many people in Oudh had acquired property by methods which the Government would never recognize that they began to fear an inquiry. Since all these people had large numbers of relations, retainers, and servants living with them, who were all interested parties, it explains the great excitement prevailing in Oudh at the time, and consequently throughout the Sirkar's army. It is my humble opinion that this seizing of Oudh filled the minds of the sepoys with distrust and led them to plot against the Government. Agents of the Nawab of Oudh and also of the King of Delhi were sent all over India to discover the temper of the army. They worked upon the feelings of the sepoys, telling them how treacherously the foreigners had behaved towards their king. They invented ten thousand lies and promises to persuade the soldiers to mutiny and turn against their masters, the English, with the object of restoring the Emperor of Delhi to the throne."

According to William Dalrymple, a major historian of the era, the annexation of Oudh was "an acquisition on a far different scale from anything yet attempted, and was practiced on 'a faithful and unresisting ally' without even the nominal justification of the absence of a recognized heir, and with only... 'fictitious charges'...as an excuse."[51] It would not be long before the son of the deposed leader of Oudh sought vengeance on the British in India.[52]

In the meantime, the British were becoming continually more complacent about their status in India. Though Dalhousie warned in his final speech as Governor-General in 1856 that "no prudent man will venture to give you assurance of continued peace,"[53] it was generally believed that the Company had things in India well in hand. When soldiers were needed to fight

[51] Ibid., 119.
[52] Sita Ram, *From Sepoy to Subedar: Being the Life and Adventures of Subedar Sita Ram a Native Officer of the Bengal Army written and related by himself.* Ed., James Lunt. (Delhi: Vikas Publications, 1873.), 161.
[53] H.G. Keene, *History of India: From the Earliest Times to the End of the Nineteenth Century*, Vol. II. (Edinburgh: John Grant, 1906), 218.

England's other wars, they could be removed from India without concern for her safety. Though "Dalhousie lost no time in entering his protest against the propriety of withdrawing British troops from India,"[54] three regiments of British troops were removed from India in 1854 to help with the war in the Crimea.[55] This made for a ratio of five sepoys to every British soldier.[56]

H.G. Keene's massive *History of India* seems to offer a half-hearted defense of Dalhousie, who attempted to warn the Court of Directors of Britain's sullied military reputation amongst the Indians, the increasing number of Indian territories under Company rule with the decreasing number of soldiers to keep peace, and the possibility of attacks from outside the empire.[57] However, he is ultimately criticized for failing to recognize the changing nature of the Sepoy troops, especially the fact that large numbers of them were of the Oudh province and high caste Hindus who now outnumbered the ever-loyal Sikhs.[58] Though there were elite Hindus, known as the Babus, who supported many of Dalhousie's reforms and the modernization of India, older Hindu elites "were alarmed and disgusted to see their young men attending debating societies, or drinking beer, and eating beef in European houses; while the followers of the prophet, even if less directly concerned, felt like a man whose neighbor's party-wall is burning."[59]

The British announced that future recruits to the Sepoy army would need to be willing to go overseas to fight for Britain, in anticipation of the new ways in which forces would need to be used. Perhaps not surprisingly, this raised serious concerns amongst the high caste sepoys; for those in the highest caste, a trip overseas would be a desecration. The declaration meant that they must lose their religious and social status to remain in the faithful employ of the British. In addition, new recruits to the army would be, as a matter of consequence, from the lower castes and without Hindu pride and reputation.[60]

In February of 1856, Viscount Canning took over after Dalhousie returned to Britain to the expectations of a future political career and a five-thousand-pound pension. Canning, as governor-general was advised by men connected to Simon Fraser, who had been assigned to the post at Delhi just two years before and was looking forward to retirement.

---

[54] Ibid.
[55] Ibid.
[56] Ibid.
[57] Ibid.
[58] Ibid., 219.
[59] Ibid., 224.
[60] Ibid., 223.

Canning

In July of that year, the Mughal Emperor Mirza Fakhru died of cholera. The emperor had been twice married, most recently at 72 years of age, and had spent his life on entertainment and lavish meals, including the consumption of 10-12 mangoes a day, that number having been reduced from his earlier days of more liberal consumption under the advice of his doctor, who had also banned the prince from consuming large quantities of spices and mango jam.[61]

---

[61] Dalrymple, 102-3.

Mirza Fakhru

Upon the death of the Mughal leader, Fraser advised that rather than allowing one of the Crown Prince's sons to be named as successor, the end of the line be declared and the princes cut off: "It appears to me inexpedient to recognize any of the sons as Heir Apparent. The princes generally are not men of prominent influence or high personal character…little public interest is felt in the fortunes of the family and a favorable opportunity is presented, by the removal from the scene of the most respected member of the family, for the introduction of changes adapted to the altered condition of the family and the Country."[62]

According to Canning's Lieutenant Governor C.B. Thornhill, Fraser's advice should be heeded as there would be "much regret if advantage were not taken of the favorable and easy opportunity now afforded for introducing a change which while it is obviously fitting in the actual condition of the Indian empire [is also] for the best interests of the princes themselves" since "the abolition of the names and forms of the royal state will, it may reasonably be hoped, wean them more readily from the habits of the idle, and too often vicious and discreditable

---

[62] Ibid., 114.

frivolities, with which their lives have hitherto been wasted."[63] Upon this advice and his own observations (despite only five months on the scene), Viscount Canning decided that it was time to end the Mughal line in Delhi: "The Upper Provinces of India are not now, as they were in 1849 or 1850, in an unsettled or uneasy condition. There is every appearance that the presence of the Royal House in Dehlie has become a matter of indifference even to the Mahometans."[64]

Mangal Pandey

The story of the Sepoy that sparked the rebellion against the British was popularized in a 2005 film. The real story of Mangal Pandey, however, would prove to be more difficult to discern. In his book *The Upside-Down Tree*, Richard Connerney describes Pandey as a common soldier under the influence of hashish, and so affected that in his suicide attempt following an attack on his commanding officers considering the greased cartridge rumor, he failed to take his own life.[65] He was hanged by the British in April of 1857. Connerney critiques the film as playing loosely with historical facts, though he credits it with an attempt at balance on the portrayal of the British soldiers and Hindus.

---

[63] Ibid., 114-115.
[64] Ibid., 116.
[65] Richard Connerney, The Upside-Down Tree: India's Changing Culture (New York: Algora, 2009), 71.

Pandey

In yet another source on Pandey, a children's book titled with his name, Pandey is lauded as a "lion amongst men…who roared just once to carve an immortal niche in history."[66] The author describes India as a place where British officers "behaved so inhumanly that Indians were like animals to them"[67] and made all decisions with the motive of controlling their growing empire. In this land where "the strength of Indian Kings and nawabs [was] significantly diminished…The entire system of the nation lay in ruins. If any class was prospering under these circumstances, it was the British class itself or the selfish Indians who were there sycophants."[68]

It is difficult to find unbiased sources regarding Pandey, who was a low-level Brahmin who joined the sepoys to escape the mounting debt of his family. In "Mangal Pandey: Drug-crazed Fanatic or Canny Revolutionary?" Professor Richard Forster attempts to find a middle ground in "the intense historiographical debate"[69] between the adulation of Indian nationalist writers and colonial accounts. First, Forster claims that Pandey likely acted with others in a planned uprising, an idea long denied by both colonial and recent historians.[70] In his "subaltern" approach to interpreting Pandey's actions, he chooses to interpret his lack of response at trial as "an indication of his connections… silence as a strategic response to specific colonialist assumptions" which "opens the way for us to at least consider the possibility that his reticence to speak at greater length at the court martial was motivated by his solidarity with the movement that was clearly swelling up beneath him, and which would project him into history."[71] Forster argues that Pandey's silence, rather than being a response to intimidation by the court-martial, was possibly "the result of an honor-bound compulsion not to implicate his fellows, "made more pressing by the presence of his peers."[72]

In attempting to place Pandey's actions in historical context, Forster cites Eric Stokes' claims that a religious explanation of the rebellion cannot be completely satisfactory since the sepoys continued to use the suspected Enfield rifle while fighting the British after the rebellion.[73] Official British records, however, account for Pandey's actions as purely religious, albeit aided by his drug-induced state. According to the official British accounts, on March 29, 1857, Pandey attempted to stir up the Sepoy regiments to which he was assigned. As the cantonment at Barrackpore awaited the arrival of a rebellious 19th regiment, which had refused to train with the supposed animal greased cartridges, Pandey called for an assembly, provoking his fellow Sepoys, "Why are you not getting ready? It is for our religion… Come out you bhainchutes, the

---

[66] Harikrishna Devsare, Mangal Pande. (Prabhat Prakashan, 2006), 1.
[67] Ibid.
[68] Ibid., 2.
[69] Richard Forster, "Mangal Pandey: Drug-crazed Fanatic or Canny Revolutionary?" The Columbia Undergraduate Journal of South Asian Studies, 4.
[70] Ibid.
[71] Ibid., 6.
[72] Ibid., 23.
[73] Ibid., 8-9.

Europeans are here. From biting these cartridges, we shall become infidels. Get ready, turn out all of you."[74] After firing upon and knifing multiple British officers, Pandey attempted to shoot himself with his rifle by using his toe, but failed. After being arrested and receiving medical assistance, Pandey was convicted by a jury of 14 natives by a vote of 11 to 3 and was hanged on April 8.

Such an "accidental hero," according to historian Rudrangshu Mukherjee, is unthinkable as the cause of the Sepoy rebellion, which did not take place until almost two months later and over a thousand miles from Barrackpore.[75] Forster takes issue with Mukherjee's thesis, pointing out that though a direct connection might not exist, small-scale mutinous acts leading to Pandey's action on April 29 seem to point to both discontent in the Sepoy army and to some form of communication that would eventually end in a larger rebellion.[76] Rather than accepting a purely religious motivation for the uprising, Foster points out the lack of camaraderie amongst the British and Indian troops that, according to the account of a Sepoy soldier who had served for over 50 years, was a rather recent development: "In those days the sahibs could speak our language much better than they do now, and they mixed more with us. Although officers today have to pass the language examination, and have to read books, they do not understand our language…The only language they learn is that of the lower orders, which they pick up from their servants, which is unsuitable to be used in polite conversation. The sahibs used to give us nautches for the regiment, and they attended all the men's games. They also took us with them when they went out hunting, or at least all those of us who wanted to go… Well, English soldiers are a different breed nowadays. They are neither as fine nor as tall as they used to be. They can seldom speak one word of our language except to abuse us and if they could learn polite expressions as quickly as they can learn abusive ones, they would indeed be apt scholars."[77]

Indeed, Dalrymple calls the British officer class "increasingly distant, rude, and dismissive" in comparison to the past. As one officer reported, he "never knew what to say" to the sepoys under his charge. This was a loss felt distinctly by the older Sepoys, who remembered "the sahibs always knew what to say, and how to say it, when I was a young soldier."[78]

Whatever the speculation of Pandey's motives, the only record of Pandey's actual words on the matter were recorded at his court martial, where he explained he had acted "of my own free will." He also said he "expected to die" and that he "had intended to take" his own life, as well as an admission of "taking bhang and opium of late, but formerly never touched any drugs. I was not aware of what I was doing."[79]

---

[74] Ibid., 10.
[75] Ibid., 11.
[76] Ibid., 15.
[77] Sitaram Pandey, qtd. In Richard Forster, 16.
[78] William Dalrymple, 128.
[79] Richard Forster, 24.

A contemporary London paper's depiction of the uprising at Meerut

An 1858 picture of a mosque at Meerut

Within two months of the incident at Barrackpore, on May 10, 1857, the outbreak of the rebellion took place at Meerut, an ancient city just under 250 miles northwest of Lucknow.[80] Indian historian Rudrangshu Mukherjee, who denies the connection between Mangal Pandey's actions months before and many hundreds of miles away, states that the mutinies in the north of India did seem to follow a pattern of outbreak from north to south, but not until the uprising at Meerut was complete.

Were there earlier signs of unrest throughout Northern India that went ignored by the British? This is a matter of great debate, and one that is still hard to definitively settle. There is evidence of small rebellious acts by several soldiers, as well as fires set between January and May, when the uprising at Meerut began. These incidents, however, can likely be explained by the growing discontent of the sepoys with conditions within the empire, including the rumors that soldiers would now have to agree to serve overseas, not to mention the persistent cartridge rumors and suspicions that religious conversions were to take place.

A persistent story in mutiny literature is that of the mysterious *chapatis*, or unleavened cakes that were thought to be passed from village to village in some kind of secret messaging system. After entertaining a number of theories regarding the *chapati*, historian Palmer concludes only that "the message of the *chapatis* was at the worst ominous, but its purport was so uncertain that

[80] Rudrangshu Mukherjee. *Awadh in Revolt, 1857-1858: A Study of Popular Resistance.* (Delhi: Permanent Black, 2001), 65.

the effect might not have been great."[81] The best historical conclusion one can draw from the recorded observations of *chapatis* in 1857, he argues, is that if they were to be at all effectual in communicating a message, there must have existed an "atmosphere of discontent" that would allow the messages a widely-understood context in Meerut and the surrounding villages.[82] The *chapatis* certainly had their effect on the British after the mutiny, as many would rue their ignorance of the ritual. As one officer recalled, "No one dreamt, like the man in Gideon's camp who saw the barley-cake overturn the tents of Midian that these farinaceous weapons were aimed at the overthrow of the British Empire in India."[83]

The cantonment at Meerut was comprised of 2,357 Indian Sepoys and 2,038 British troops, making the ratios of Britons to natives much closer than in other places throughout India. This fact has been cited by some commentators as proof that the rebellion in Meerut was spontaneous rather than planned, as many other cantonments might have served as a better place to start a premeditated national rebellion. On April 24, the British commander ordered the parading of the sepoys stationed at Meerut as a sign of obedience regarding the use of the Enfield rifle and cartridges, which had been rumored to contain animal fat.

In J.A.B. Palmer's *The Mutiny Outbreak at Meerut in 1857,* the author makes the case that the issue of greased cartridges was a false one, that the type of cartridge grease being used had been present for over a decade, and that the concerns of the sepoys had been addressed by the officers numerous times. This included good faith offers, Palmer claims, to have the sepoys manufacture their own grease, as well as instructions for tearing the cartridges with the hands and not the mouth. Other historians offer the explanation that while the initial cartridges indeed contained animal fat, the situation was quickly rectified, and the sepoys, who detested the heavily greased cartridge packages no matter the content, were making their "own lubricant of beeswax and ghee."[84] As one commentator theorized, perhaps it was that this "concession and manipulation allayed any one fear about the Enfield-Pritchett cartridge, but I suspect it was this willingness to change the drill manual and to allow the men to supply their own grease that strengthened the latter's uneasiness."[85] Here, Palmer is in agreement with Sita Ram's observations that the "very reading out of this order was seized upon by many as proof that the Sirkar had broken our caste, since otherwise the order would never have been issued. What was the use of a denial if it had not been the Government's intention originally to break our caste?"[86] As Palmer explains, the sepoys at Meerut were very connected to their families and to the social implications of the caste system. Their concerns were not primarily "personal defilement," but what would occur if they were believed to be handling items that would cause them to considered "*badnam* (of ill repute)": "[M]y good social standing will be destroyed, my comrades will have nothing to do

[81] J.A.B. Palmer, *The Mutiny Outbreak at Meerut in 1857.* (Cambridge: Cambridge university Press), 4.
[82] Ibid., 5.
[83] Mowbray Thompson, *The Story of Cawnpore.* (London: Richard Bentley, 1859), 24.
[84] William Dalrymple 126.
[85] Goldman, Robert. *Journal of the American Oriental Society* 87, no. 3 (1967): 340-43. doi:10.2307/597747.
[86] Sita Ram, 162.

with me, my family and my home will turn me away…"[87]

Historians who favor the view that religion, not purely social standing, was the greatest factor in the uprising explain that the sepoys saw the cartridges as "far from accidental" and instead a way to trick the soldiers into breaking caste, leaving them with few options but conversion to Christianity. By 1857, though far fewer of the Meerut Sepoys could claim a high caste (about 65% compared to 80% elsewhere), only just above one percent were Christian. In the face of increasing western influence, some sepoys were affected by "sanskritisination," or increased attention to dietary and religious purity laws that set them apart from lower caste members in the force.[88] As Sita Ram describes the rumors, "the great aim of the English was to turn us all into Christians, and they had therefore introduced the cartridge in order to bring this about, since both Mahommedans and Hindus would be defiled by using it."[89]

In early May, signs of serious discontent and possible rebellion were showing at Meerut. Secret meetings of the Bengals took place, at which point the commanding officers began to communicate their concerns with the commander in chief, Lord Clyde. Graffiti began to appear; slogans which called for unity or an end to obedience of the British were an obvious call for alarm. An account of the Meerut and Delhi uprisings by John Edward Wharton Rotton, a chaplain to both areas of India was recorded at first "for the perusal of none but himself,"[90] but later published as *The Chaplain's Narrative of the Siege of Delhi*. Rotton describes the sepoys as suddenly rejecting the cartridges they had used previously without complaint. Thus, 85 men were arrested, convicted, and sentenced, with the longest term of punishment being 10 years.

The following morning, May 9, the convicts were brought out to the parade ground where they were placed in irons in front of the Sepoy troops and their sentences read aloud. The chaplain describes a time of quiet following the incarceration of the 85, but a warning delivered on the morning of May 10 by a servant girl that the family should not attend church services that day because the sepoys "would fight."[91] Despite the warning, the chaplain attended services with his family and servant with only a walking cane as a potential weapon, the only one he ever carried or believed he would need to, according to his diary. Nonetheless, after describing the outbreak at Meerut, which he knew only too soon was real, Rotton lays out his belief that the Meerut outbreak was a mistake —a too early action in a wider plot that existed, "a day was fixed upon, in the counsel of the mutineers, for the massacre of every European and Christian person in India."[92]

Chaplain Rotton describes the carnage visible in Meerut by Monday morning after a day of

---

[87] J.A.B. Palmer, 6.
[88] William Dalrymple, 126.
[89] Sita Ram, 162.
[90] John Edward Wharton Rotton, *The Chaplain's Narrative of the Siege of Delhi*. (London: Smith, Elder, and Company, 1858), v.
[91] Ibid., 3.
[92] Ibid., 5.

waiting safely protected by the British troops available for his protection: "What spectacles of terror met the eye almost simultaneously with the return of the day! The lifeless and mutilated corpses of men, women, and children were here and there to be seen, some of them so frightfully disfigured and so shamefully dishonored in death, that the very recognition of such sights chills the blood, and makes one rue the day that ever dawned upon such scenes of merciless carnage."[93]

In the heat and dryness of May in India, the structures that housed British officers and families, as well as the garrisons of British troops were easily put to fire.[94] A British soldier's account of the uprising at Meerut was published in the *Cheltenham Looker-On*, and in it he described the terrible aftermath of the uprising, with British soldiers being sent out on vengeance missions daily following the rebellion. He calls the missions "butcher's work —burn villages and slaughter the population, and I rejoice at its being done, though I should not like the work."[95]

Spread of the Mutiny

The Sepoy Mutiny, whatever its ultimate cause, remained largely isolated to Northern India, spreading from Meerut to Delhi, Cawnpore, Lucknow, Jhansi, Indore, Punjab and Arrah. Though outbreaks happened in places other than those discussed below, they were limited to local disturbances put down quickly by the British forces. In all, the mutiny lasted just over two years, and it permanently changed the relationship between the British and the people of India. To understand the scope of the mutiny, as well as its impact on the relations between colonizer and colonized, it's necessary to review the events of the uprising in various northern regions.

Delhi

The mutineers themselves, according to Rotton, had moved from Meerut to Delhi without the slightest response from the British, who were overwhelmed and surprised into inaction. Instead, they arrived at Delhi with that city unprepared for the fight as well. The sepoys sought the blessing of the Mughal Emperor of Delhi, Bahadur Shah Zafar. At 82, he had "little choice" but to join with the mutineers since the British were already fleeing the city. Though Zafar first told the mutineers that they had "acted wickedly," their insistence (and proximity) made Zafar "like the king on the chessboard after the checkmate."[96] Zafar agreed to bless the rebel sepoys.

---

[93] Ibid., 6.
[94] John Keay, 438.
[95] "Meerut." *The Cheltenham Looker-On.* September 26, 1857.
[96] William Dalrymple, 161-162.

Zafar

Though Zafar's part in the mutiny could be said to be accidental, it lent a political nature to the rebellion,[97] and perhaps gave it more greater seriousness in the eyes of many, both Indian and British. In fact, in "combining the company's own Indian armies with the still potent mystique of the Mughals, Zafar's hesitant acceptance of the nominal leadership of the revolt…turned it from a simple army mutiny—albeit one supported by an incoherent eruption of murder and looting by Delhi's civilians— into the single most serious armed challenge any western empire would face, anywhere in the world, in the entire course of the nineteenth century."[98]

Taking most of the day to do their work, the sepoys fell upon the Cashmere Gate with a great number of men, aided, according to Rotton, by the sepoys inside. Rotton records that in Meerut there was no assistance of any sepoy in aide of a British officer or civilian, and that each sepoy joined in the killings and helped the movement of the mutineers into the city gates. Rotton's conclusions about Indian loyalty were clearly incorrect, though it is understandable that in the mayhem taking place at Meerut, it may have looked as if every Indian soldier was intent on killing or allowing the death of the Europeans.

---

[97] John Keay, 439.
[98] William Dalrymple, 179.

A depiction of the attack on the Cashmere Gate

A picture of mortar damage done to the gate

The newly "empowered" Zafar was to set up a council, and the invigorated Delhi civilians began to align themselves behind him. This was no longer simply a military mutiny.[99] On May 17, a Delhi newspaper celebrated the victory over the English: "Truly the English have been afflicted with divine wrath the true avenger. Their arrogance has brought them divine retribution, for as the Holy Koran says, 'God does not love the arrogant ones.' God has given the Christians such a body blow that within a short time this carnage has utterly destroyed them...It is now incumbent on you, people of Delhi, to have faith in God and all those who should expose all their energy in protecting and being loyal to the shadow of God on earth, his exalted Majesty (the Emperor Bahadur Shah Zafar)."

British officers outside the city commanded their usually loyal sepoys to return to their barracks, or to drill, but they were ignored as the news that British rule was soon to end spread quickly. When the sepoys saw the smoke rising from Delhi and heard loud explosions coming from the city, some simply fled their camps. British officers and their families congregated at the Flagstaff Tower, awaiting news about their men. A cart of British bodies arrived at the tower, creating a "stampede" to flee the tower and escape the advancing sepoys.[100] Those at the main guard area just inside the main gate of the city were massacred by 200 sepoys, with only ten survivors, who escaped by jumping into a 25-foot ditch and scrambling up the other side to safety. These were pursued throughout the night until they made plans to escape Delhi and head toward Meerut to seek safety there.

The Flagstaff Tower where the Europeans gathered on May 11 for protection

---

[99] Ibid.
[100] William Dalrymple, 165-7.

Another historian records a debate between two sepoys about the attacks on British officers, wives, and children. In answer to the other's argument that if all the English were to be put to death, there would be no employment, the soldier replied that the new King of Delhi would supply jobs and wages for all.[101]

On May 12, Delhi was "almost completely emptied of the British" for the first time since 1803.[102] It would take Britain time to organize their troops, as they were forced to bring some from England and Persia, divert some who were en route to nearby Asian destinations, and to reorganize those in the field.[103] The fight over Delhi lasted two months, with the British forces outside the city attempting to retake it and the Indians inside attempting organization. By September, when the British were able to retake the city, fresh bloodshed began. Zafar was exiled to Rangoon, while three of his heirs were killed in escape attempts.[104]

The rebellion in Delhi, despite its temporary success and its death toll, did not spark a national rebellion, but it continued to feed a regional one. It is important to note that the armies of both Bombay and Madras remained loyal to the English throughout the mutiny.[105] Even in the north, many kingdoms remained loyal, or at least neutral, in the uprising.

[101] Ibid., 176.
[102] Ibid., 177.
[103] New World Encyclopedia contributors, "Indian Rebellion of 1857," *New World Encyclopedia*, http://www.newworldencyclopedia.org/p/index.php?title=Indian_Rebellion_of_1857&oldid=980264 (accessed November 13, 2016).
[104] Ibid.
[105] John Keay, 440.

A depiction of mutineers attacking British families

Lucknow and the Siege of Cawnpore

A depiction of mutineers attacking a redan at Lucknow

If any exception to the more limited definition of the uprising exists, it would be in Oudh (Awadh), the site of both the siege of Cawnpore and the Battle of Lucknow. It is here, argues author John Keay, that the mutiny could truly be said to be one of the people, and not just a military or political rebellion. As one of the stronger kingdoms, Oudh had only recently been annexed under the new policies of the British government, so resentment was fresh. The fact that the Sepoy armies had always drawn heavily on Oudh for recruiting soldiers meant that a third of the army's soldiers hailed from Oudh.[106]

Lucknow was the capital of the region. Dalhousie had refused to accept Nana Sahib, an adopted heir, as the legitimate ruler of Oudh and annexed the country he called "a disgrace to our empire" against the advice of some of his subordinates, in 1856.[107] There is no question of Nana Sahib's lavish and extravagant lifestyle, or of his neglect of the people he ruled, but many felt that the "weak, harmless prince, who had done the British no injury, but like his ancestors, had ever been faithful to them" should have been allowed to remain.

After the British retook Delhi and deposed Zafar in September, the city of Lucknow became the center of the uprising. The disgraced Nana Sahib became the new face of the rebellion, and he took on the role, though some might speculate unwillingly.

---

[106] Ibid.
[107] Ibid., 433-435.

Known today as Kanpur, the city of Cawnpore lay just 50 miles from Lucknow. Taking refuge from the spreading rebellion in a British garrison under the direction of General John Wheeler were 240 men, and 375 women and children, a number which included sepoys who remained loyal to the British despite the growing mutiny. In a soldier's account of Cawnpore, he called Wheeler not only "one of the most distinguished generals of the Company's army," but also "perfectly powerless…broken down from over exertion and anxiety of the mind."[108] Wheeler devised a plan to build an entrenchment in which the British officers and their families, as well as those loyal to the British would stay, storing away provisions that would last the group for weeks. One officer later described the British as "defended simply by a low mud wall, barely four feet high with a shallow ditch, not worthy the name of entrenchments."[109] There was division amongst the officer corps about the wisdom of this plan. Some in the British military leadership believed the magazine should have been the chosen spot of refuge, and some officers and their families left Cawnpore, believing that the risk of staying was greater than being killed by mutineers. These officers thought that if they could make it to Lucknow, where they assumed the British still would have things well in hand, or to bungalows outside of the city, they would be safe. Instead, those who left the entrenchments and were captured were killed outright or brought to Nana Sahib, who "put them to the sword."[110]

Of course, those who remained with the garrison in the entrenchment had no idea of their fellow soldiers' fates at the time. In fact, Wheeler trusted Nana Sahib, and believed that he would remain loyal in defending the British there if given the right incentives. Thus, he offered Nana Sahib access to Cawnpore's ammunition stores and treasury.[111] Wheeler believed the Nana Sahib would be faithful and was encouraged in this belief by his wife, who knew Sahib personally and convinced her husband that he represented no danger. It was widely understood that, if the mutiny came to Cawnpore, the natives would empty the treasury and move on to another city.[112]

Instead, on the 6th of June, when the sepoys at the garrison of Cawnpore mutinied, Nana Sahib gave himself over to the mutineers, now led by the former head of Nana Sahib's kitchens, Tatya Tope. Sahib, threatened with death if he refused to serve as their leader, but promised a great Kingdom for leading the mutineers, is said to have made his decision in retribution for his lost pension. "What have I to do with the British?" he said, "I am yours."[113] Sepoy witnesses would claim that Nana Sahib regretted the treachery but did not stop it when it came. Despite the fact that he had given his word to Wheeler, Nana Sahib's brother, an even "greater villain," claimed that he and his men were free from any promises.[114]

---

[108] W.J. Shepherd. A Personal Narrative of the Outbreak and Massacre at Cawnpore During the Sepoy Revolt of 1857. (Cawnpore: London Printing Press, 1879), 55.

[109] Ibid., 73.

[110] Ibid., 57.

[111] Bruce Watson, The Great Indian Mutiny: Colin Campbell and the Campaign at Lucknow (New York: Praeger Publishers, 1991), 62.

[112] W.J. Shepherd, A Personal Narrative of the Outbreak and Massacre at Cawnpore, During the Sepoy Revolt of 1857. (Lucknow: London Printing Press, 1879), 7-9.

[113] John Keay, 442.

W.J. Shepherd, a soldier at the garrison, recorded gaining permission from General Wheeler to leave the entrenchment and seek news of Lucknow and Allahabad. Shepherd describes disguising himself as a Sepoy cook, but he was nevertheless captured and brought to the Nana Sahib. Here, he was questioned about the status of the British garrison in the entrenchment, how many men were still alive, and how much longer they could survive the siege of the mutineers. Under instructions from Wheeler, Shepherd replied that the garrison had enough supplies to last another month (though conditions inside were reaching desperation) and that the British fully expected reinforcements to arrive soon.

Wheeler, now holed up in the British garrison and realizing Nana Sahib's new position, nevertheless took Sahib at his word when, on June 24, he offered the prisoners safe passage downriver to Allahabad. The terms were delivered by a female prisoner of the mutineers in a note purported to be from Nana Sahib himself: "All those who are in noway [sic] connected with the acts of Lord Dalhousie, and are willing to lay down their arms, shall receive a safe passage to Allahabad."[115] Wheeler rejected this first message, demanding that it be properly addressed and signed, and that Nana Sahib send representatives to discuss the terms of the emptying of the British garrison. The agreement stipulated that the wounded and sick, women, and children would be allowed to reach covered boats under no attack, that the boats would be supplied with food and water, and that the men who were able would leave the entrenchment with their weapons and 60 rounds of ammunition each.[116] The British were allowed to prepare for their journey under the cessation of fire by the mutineers, and washed and dressed for the first time in 20 days. Access to water had been restricted because of the placement of the entrenchments. The only water source had exposed those seeking it to Sepoy fire.

After sending a team of British men to inspect the boats that would take them on their course, the British began to be escorted onto ships on the morning of June 27. One Colonel Williams mused, "A truly sad spectacle it must have been to see that noble little band, that had for twenty long days, in the hottest season of the year, kept at bay their numerous bloodthirsty foes… and yielding only at last from compassion to the weak and helpless innocents whose sole reliance was their brave hearts and sturdy arms, with a vain hope of shortening their sufferings and securing their retreat—sturdy men, delicate women that had never hitherto known an hour's of privation—tenderly brought up children, whose every want had been anticipated, —sad, indeed, must it have been to see them now reduced by privation, soiled with unremitting labour, and the absence even of the common necessaries of life, scorched by an Indian sun and the fierce simoon, tattered and torn, weak and wounded, hastening on with eager steps and beating hearts, to the cruel fate awaiting them, all unconscious of the base treachery planned by their foes for their destruction."[117]

---

[114] W.J. Shepherd, 82.
[115] Ibid., 71.
[116] Ibid., 72.
[117] Colonel Williams, qtd. In W.J. Shepherd, 73.

As 450 British men, women, and children drew near the banks of the river, the treachery had already begun at the now occupied garrison. Those who were most severely sick and wounded were to be sent for with "doolies" that would allow them to be carried once the others had reached the boats. These 12 were then slaughtered by the sepoys as the others marched on unaware. Gunfire was heard "even before that doomed little band had reached that fatal spot" where their ships were to be set off and lit afire.[118]

At 9:00, a bugle call sounded, and the sepoys opened fire with rifles and cannon that had been prepared on the roof of a nearby home. Those anxious to impress the new leadership of the mutiny under Nana Sahib showed their commitment to the cause by murdering the men, women, and children who they had recently served. The boats, some already on the river, were lit afire with their thatched roofs, leaving the injured and sick to burn to death and those with the ability to do so to jump into the river. Here, they either drowned or were killed by sepoys or villagers (who had lined the banks to watch) with swords, knives, and clubs.[119] General Wheeler's daughter supposedly saved herself by recalling to the sepoy, who threatened her, her father's position as his commanding officer and the many kindnesses that he had received at his hand. As the account goes, however, she was killed seconds later by a villager who clubbed her to death.[120]

Some argue that the majority of mutineers, though willing to join in the rebellion, had no intention of carrying out the slaughter as planned and refused to do so. Instead, they were confused when some of Nana Sahib's own men fired upon the British. For his part, Nana Sahib ordered an end to the slaughter only after all the men had been killed. This included the sons of the British, even infants, who were said to be "torn in two" and thrown into the river, and the older boys who were killed with rifles or bayonets.[121] At the same time, Nana Sahib realized that the 130 mother and daughter survivors were witnesses to the murders, and began to fear the retribution of the British. For those that ascribe to this theory, as the death count mounted, the need to rid Cawnpore of the British completely, as well as all evidence of what had taken place, became paramount. It was known that a British force was within 15 miles of the city. The sepoys were ordered to enter Bibighar, the house in which the women and female children were being held, and shoot the survivors before the arrival of the British. However, the soldiers sent to perform this task refused to do so. The source of the subsequent order was said to be a female attendant charged with the care of the British females. Five men from the town, including two local butchers, slaughtered the women and children, whose bodies were then thrown in the well behind Bibighar.[122] General Havelock, after he finally arrived, discovered the bodies and the

---

[118] George W. Forrest, ed., *The Indian Mutiny 1757-1758: Selections from the Letters, Dispatches, and Other State Papers Preserved in the Military Department of the Government of India.* Volume III. (New Delhi: Asian Educational Services, 2000), Appendix.

[119] W.J. Shepherd, 76.

[120] Ibid., 77.

[121] Ibid.

[122] Bruce Allen Watson, *When Soldiers Quit: Studies in Military Disintegration* (Westport, CT: Praeger Publishers,

evidence of what had taken place inside Bibighar. Upon the discovery of body parts, blood, and human hair, it was said that "stalwart, bearded men, stern soldiers of the ranks ... have been seen coming out of that house perfectly unmanned, utterly unable to repress their emotions."[123]

The site of the well

As word of Bibighar leaked to other Indian cities and to Britain itself, Europeans were aghast. Tales of Bibighar fueled violent retribution in the four days that followed the discovery as natives were rounded up and those found to be responsible were tried and executed. Some of the convicted were made to lick the blood off the floors of Bibighar just prior to their deaths, and locals who had refused to come to the aide of the women were hanged in sight of the Cawnpore well. Throughout 1858, the British sought both revenge and to leave no doubt in the minds of the natives just who oversaw the continent. Lord Canning had passed Act XIV of 6th June 1857 after the outbreak of the rebellion. It "made 'exciting mutiny or sedition in the army' a crime punishable by death" and was to last for one year.[124] It was this act that gave the legal power to British armies for the deaths of so many natives.

Much of the immediate response consisted of calls for revenge and of paintings, poems, and tales of violence perpetrated against innocent victims, much of which heavily implied that the women of Bibighar had been sexually assaulted before the killings, an idea later proven largely

---

1997), 34.
[123] Alex Tickell. "Cawnpore, Kipling and Charivari: 1857 and the politics of commemoration." *Literature and History*, 18(2) 2009, 2.
[124] Ibid., 8.

unsubstantiated. With the passage of some time, some commentators, including one soldier, George Smith of the 46th regiment, recalled the incident as the horrible result of a lack of watchfulness and care, perpetrated by the desire for profits and empire under the British East India Company. In his poem, "The Well at Cawnpore," published in the January 30, 1875 edition of the *Maitland Mercury*, Smith makes the accusations clear:

"O why with death's dark trappings bound,

And pealing anthem's plaintive sound,

Seek ye to consecrate the ground

Already consecrated

With the best blood of those who found

In the deep dark well's circle round,

Beneath yon piled up grassy mound,

A rest for souls belated!

Ye but renew the anguish deep,

Worn hearts felt once, as thus ye creep

Around the spot where sad souls weep

And wailing tell

How dear ones fell

In Cawnpore's corpse-encumbered well!

O cease the plaintive strain, forbear

To march with humble, contrite air.

Around the slender structure fair,

With miens all meek and lowly,

The ground ye tread, yon temple rare,

Were consecrated by despair!

By woman's blood shed wanton there!

Oh God! The place is holy!

And ye, oh! had ye but been wise,

And heeded caution's warning cries,

Such deeds had never shamed the skies

As here befell,

Nor could men tell

How treason filled yon dark deep well.

When first the dreadful whisper ran,

That blanched the cheeks of beauty wan,

How treason numbered off its clan,

And souls with fear benighted

Shrank as they listened to the plan

Of those who, in the rebel van,

The Lotus pass'd from man to man,

E'en then was caution slighted!

Great Mammon's gains ye still pursued.

And all life's pleasing pleasures wooed,

And muttered, "Madness! folly rude!

Your terrors quell,

They'll ne'er rebel!

They answered ye with this dark well!

To false conclusions thus ye leapt!

And weakly, blindly, madly slept,

While cruel treason onward crept,

Red-handed! stony-hearted!!

Forewarned, alas! 'e'en then ye slept

Not in, while even manhood wept

O'er every joy in life bereft.

And love for aye departed!

The hand was raised to strike the blow,

Yet still ye said, "Rebellion, no!"

'Tis but weak woman's fears!' when, Io!

'Neath Murder's yell

The red hand fell!

Survey its work in Cawnpore's well!"

The poem was written by Smith, who attended the commissioning of a formal memorial to the victims of the Bibighar murders. The memorial consisted of the statue of an angel surrounded by octagonal stone walls and a landscaped park. Here, the British only (as natives were banned from visiting for many years) could come to remember those they had lost and to be reinvigorated in their sobriety about the need to control native populations for the indefinite future.[125]   After India gained its independence, the "Ladies' Memorial" erected at Bibighar was vandalized and replaced with a statue of the leader of the massacre's aftermath, Tatya Tope.[126]

---

[125] Ibid., 10.
[126] "Mutiny in the Empire." *The Telegraph.* 31 August 1996.

The memorial to the victims

An illustration depicting Tope

At the end of June, Lucknow had been captured by the mutineers, and the British soldiers, their faithful Indian counterparts, and nearly 144 women, children, and servants sheltered just outside the city. Their stand led to a 5-month long siege that, unlike Cawnpore, ended with success. Historian John Keay contends that though Cawnpore was taboo, "Lucknow was a soaring triumph of spirit, eminently worth mythologizing, and defiantly commemorated by the Union Jack, which would fly, night and day, above the ravaged Residency for the remaining ninety years of British rule." The city of Lucknow remained in rebel hands until March of 1858; its fall signaled the beginning of the end for the mutineers' cause.

Jhansi

Dalhousie had annexed Jhansi in 1853, refusing to accept the young ruler, an adopted son of the dead king. The king's widow, Lakshmibai, however, proved a powerful and attractive leader, and a story similar to Cawnpore began to unfold. Though not actively seeking a following, Lakshmibai was co-opted by the mutineers at Jhansi.[127] When a group of British soldiers and families accepted her promise of safe passage, they too were slaughtered by Sepoy troops. This left Lakshmibai "implicated and defenseless," though the British were too preoccupied to

---

[127] John Keay, 443.

immediately respond.

Seizing an opportunity, two rival groups attacked Jhansi, challenging Lakshmibai and prodding many soldiers and locals coming to her defense. Lakshmibai attempted to contact the British, writing of her loyalty and her desire to separate herself from the acts of violence perpetrated on the British soldiers and citizens in Jhansi. With no response from the Company other than the British Bombay army converging on Jhansi in early 1858, Lakshmibai now turned to one who she believed would protect her position, Tatya Tope, fresh from the Cawnpore massacre.

Though he ultimately failed to protect Jhansi from the British siege in March of 1858, his response gave Lakshmibai time to escape the city in disguise. She and Tatya Tope met up in Gwalior, a city called "the heights of Abraham" for its excellent position and a stronghold for the mutiny, where they would fight the British another day.[128] On the first day of the fight, Lakshmibai was killed by British fire while inspecting the walls of the city. Her magnetism as a leader led to comparisons to Joan of Arc, Jezebel, and as one British soldier called her in a telling

[128] John Keay, 443-44.

tribute, "the only man amongst the rebels."[129] Today, Indian nationalists recall Lakshmibai as a great feminist hero, and she is popularized in literature, children's stories, and song. Several schools and universities in India also bear her name.

After the death of Lakshmibai, the mutiny began to lose its strength. Though there were certainly more fights and more deaths to come, the never well-organized sepoy forces had lost momentum, and rival power groups within Indian Kingdoms now sought to use the upheaval to advance their own interests. As one historian described the mutiny, "Far from being a coordinated movement, it was a series of uprisings, their volatility dependent on local circumstances."[130] These circumstances began to work against the mutineers in the second half of 1858, though they continued to hold out against the British in pockets of resistance.

Indore

At Indore, Colonel Durand had refused to consider that his station, like those before, would mutiny. Though he had been pressed upon by some of his men to take precautions, Durand felt it best to maintain an air of confident control. On the morning of July 1, 1858, however, Durand contacted nearby Mhow to request a battery for his defense. A force that he had requested in the defense of the British residency was now attacking it. When his cavalry officers led a charge against the advancing force, the British officers were shocked to find only a few Sikh troops obeyed orders. The infantry not only refused to fight, but turned their weapons upon their officers, emboldened by the presence of a mutinous display.[131] Durand, knowing what was to come, determined that he had no choice but to flee Indore. "Finding", he wrote, "that the cavalry who were loyal, though disordered and out of control, would be off on their own score, I very unwillingly gave the order to retire; and, mounting the ladies on the gun wagons, we made an orderly retreat, bringing off every European that had not killed during the first surprise."[132] Altogether about 39 of Durand's residency were killed in the uprising. Durand ruefully reflected on his retreat, which he considered the most bitter act of his lifetime: "...We retired unmolested in the face of superior masses, whose appetite for blood had been whetted by the murder of unarmed men, women, and children... I had never had to retreat, still less to order a retreat myself...I would have been thankful had anyone shot me."[133]

Punjab

In Punjab, a large administrative region that contained the greatest ratio of European troops to natives, a telegram had been received warning British officers of an impending strike.

[129] Ibid., 444.
[130] Bruce Watson, The Great Indian Mutiny: Colin Campbell and the Campaign at Lucknow (New York: Praeger Publishers, 1991), 65.
[131] John William Kaye, 330-332.
[132] Ibid., 332.
[133] Ibid., 333.

Immediately, the officers began to organize a force, a "double line" with which to respond to the mutiny in progress. As John Nicholson, a deputy commissioner and soldier in the Punjab put it, "mutiny is a smallpox" that must be responded to and put down immediately, before its spread made it too difficult to contain.[134] Nicholson argued "neither greased cartridges, the annexation of Oude, nor the paucity of European officers were the causes [of rebellion]. For years, I have watched the army and felt sure they only wanted the opportunity to try their strength with us."

The officers in Punjab called for European forces to respond initially, and they also began to assemble those Indians who they believed would remain loyal to the British—mainly Sikhs and Muslims, whom they believed would have little in common with the Hindu soldiers.[135] In all, over 34,000 Sikhs were brought into the Company armies after the outbreak of rebellion. This meant that though outbreaks would continue to occur in the region, they could be put down quickly and their spread became less likely.

The End of Rebellion

With the Government of India Act, issued in 1858, the East India Company was liquidated and the British crown became the administrators of what was now the British Empire in India. Though the company had been losing privileges with each successive re-charter of its rights, the rebellion ensured that the Company itself would exist no longer than 1874.[136] In place of Company directors, the British would rule India directly, through a governor-general appointed by the British Secretary for India and his council.[137] Lord Canning, having arrived in India just two years before the mutiny, would serve in the new capacity until 1862.

Canning, in his day, was criticized by many for both his lack of awareness regarding the impending revolt and, later, his leniency on the native populations after the rebellion. Canning was not necessarily a friend of the natives, but he believed that further reprisals would make it harder to rule the country and bring things more quickly back under Britain's control. For example, Canning considered the natives of Oudh to be ungrateful for the liberation the British had attempted to bestow on them by the annexation and removal of the claimant to the Mughal throne. Frustrated, he wrote, "Their conduct almost amounts to the admission that their own rights, whatever these may be, are subordinate to those of the Talookdar; that they do not value the recognition of these rights by the ruling authority; and that the Talookdaree system is the ancient, indigenous, and cherished system of the country."[138]

Nonetheless, Canning knew that loyal princes who had refused to take part in the mutiny and instead supported their British funders had functioned as "breakwaters to the storm which would

---

[134] Charles Allen, Soldier Sahibs: The Daring Adventurers Who Tamed India's Northwest Frontier. (New York: Carroll and Graf Publishers, 2000), 266.
[135] Ibid.260-266.
[136] "East India Company and Raj 1785-1858" About Parliament. www.parliament.uk
[137] Ibid.
[138] Thomas R. Metcalf. Ideologies of the Raj, Volume 3, Part 4 (New York: Cambridge University Press, 1995), 46.

have otherwise swept over us in one great wave."[139] The British acted out of a policy of reward and punishment, giving titles, land, and rights to those who had been loyal during the rebellion. Canning also offered an amendment to the Act IV, which had allowed any acts against the British government during the war to be punishable by death. The clemency resolution promised forgiveness to sepoys within a rebelling regiment if they had personally protected their officers and not engaged in "heinous crime against person or property." By stating that he was "anxious to prevent measures of extreme severity," he earned the derisive nickname "Clemency Canning."[140]

The Sepoy Rebellion was a regional phenomenon, but it had implications for all of India as over a century of Company rule was replaced by a more formal relationship with the crown and direct rule, subject not only to the profit motive but to political motivations as well. The story of the Raj would come next, and India would both benefit and suffer under the administration of the British until 1947.

In the meantime, the blood that had been shed along the Ganges flowed throughout India, bringing with it continued tension, conflicting policies, and religious resentments. Though the British had been successful at avoiding a full-scale war of independence in 1857, they would be out of India completely in less than 100 years.

The New India

Once it had put a stop to the rebellion by defeating the various Indian rebel groups individually,[141] the British government ended up ruling India directly. However, as McLeod pointed out, "Like much of British imperial expansion, taking formal control of India was not intentional. Instead when British lives and trading interests (represented by the East India Company) were threatened by violent reaction to encroaching westernization, London felt obligated to step in to take control of both the situation and the country."[142] The news was delivered to the Indian people in a proclamation by the English government in 1858.[143]

At the highest levels, the new administrative structure of India was out of the new India Office and headed, at home, by the Secretary of State for India. In India, a new title–viceroy–was added to the position of governor-general, signifying that the authority now held the weight of the crown.[144]

Why did the British desire to continue their reign in India despite the bloody rebellion of 1857?

---

[139] Ibid., 191.
[140] Christopher Herbert, *War of No Pity: The Indian Mutiny and Victorian Trauma.* (Princeton: Princeton University Press, 2008), 106.
[141] John McLeod, 83.
[142] Robert Carr, "Concession & Repression: British Rule in India 1857-1919: Robert Carr Assesses the Nature of British Rule in India during a Key, Transitional Phase," *History Review*, no. 52 (2005).
[143] Sneh Mahajan, British Foreign Policy, 1874-1914: The Role of India (London: Routledge, 2002), 37.
[144] McLeod, 83.

McLeod cautions against a too ready acceptance of any single purpose. Rather than seeing India as a purely economic venture or only a source of international empire, the British desired to keep India within the empire for multiple and changing reasons. Certainly, there were economic benefits for Britain, as 25% of Indian taxes ended up in the mother country for administrative purposes, retirement pensions for former Indian officers, and as interest on loans made to India.[145] Acknowledging the economic factors, however, should not allow for the discounting of others, including Britain's desire to maintain her holdings in the East; to influence India religiously, educationally, and culturally; and to maintain her own image as a dominant power.[146]

Though the proposal was raised far earlier in 1858, it was not until 1877 that Queen Victoria was named the "Empress of India," in a ceremony held in Delhi.[147] The interest in expansion of nations like Russia, Austria, and a relatively new German nation-state eager to make a reputation, led Victoria to believe the title of empress would raise her status from "petulant widow to imperial matriarch."[148] These "psychological" concerns must weigh as heavily as the economic ones in understanding the desire for continued British dominance of India.

---

[145] Ibid., 84.
[146] Ibid.
[147] Sneh Mahajan.
[148] Ibid.

Queen Victoria

A formal portrait of Victoria as Empress of India

An Indian coin depicting the queen

Though it had been decided that the rule of India would continue under the Raj, the way in which the relationship between Britain and India would be viewed had yet to be determined. For many British thinkers, the mutiny "left a lasting mark on both the style and the ideology of British rule."[149] Though the liberals believed India could be westernized and modernized through a combination of education and political cooperation, based on "the gratitude and appreciation of the ruled…These beliefs had proved to be illusions."[150] Instead, the bloody mutiny confirmed in the minds of many Brits that India was and would remain a group destined for Western subjugation, ruled, albeit benevolently, by racial superiors. Albertini and Wirz explain, "This was henceforth the ideological basis of the British Raj. Although the other things the English brought India–domestic peace, a unified legal system, and modern administration–were also considered to legitimize British rule, the implicit or stated conviction remained, that India now "belonged" to England and that Indians were incompetent to rule themselves or manage their own affairs; as indeed were all nonwhite races."[151]

The India Office understood the need to avoid another rebellion, and they also knew that to rule British India effectively, it must have the support of nearly the whole land. Thus, the British increased the presence of British officers in India, but also concentrated on making alliances with Indian rulers in non-British regions of India, who were guaranteed their lands would never be annexed by the Crown in return for their loyalty. In its 1858 Royal Message, it was declared "that the British 'desire no extension of [our] present territorial possession and would respect the rights, dignity and honour of the native princes as our own.' States and territories, large and

---

[149] Rudolf Von Albertini and Albert Wirz, European Colonial Rule, 1880-1940: The Impact of the West on India, Southeast Asia, and Africa, trans. John G. Williamson (Westport, CT: Greenwood Press, 1982), 7.
[150] Ibid., 8.
[151] Ibid.

small, that had come under British rule during the expansionist phase as a result of protectorate and subsidiary treaties, retained the same status."[152] Those who had remained faithful to Britain during the rebellion were highly rewarded.[153]

To aid in the rule of the Indian people, the British established a new Indian Civil Service with a dedication to maintaining and promoting fair policy and rooting out corrupt practices.[154] The Civil Service employed British officers, but also many Indian civil servants who worked in India's provinces. The officers were described by one British-Indian writer as "minutely just, scrupulously honest, and inflexibly upright, introducing the culture and tradition of impartial and good governance without corruption."[155] The Indian Civil Service, which commentator after commentator mentions as an astounding example of fair and peaceful rule of many by the few, soon became known as "the steel frame" of India.[156]

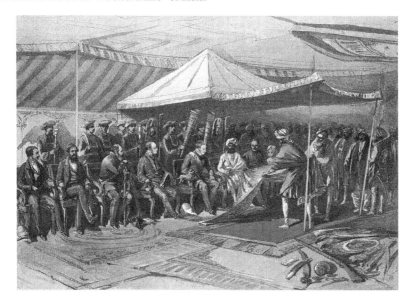

A depiction of Viceroy Lord Canning meeting Maharaja Ranbir Singh of Jammu & Kashmir in March 1860

[152] Rudolf Von Albertini and Albert Wirz, European Colonial Rule, 1880-1940: The Impact of the West on India, Southeast Asia, and Africa, trans. John G. Williamson (Westport, CT: Greenwood Press, 1982), 12.
[153] McLeod, 85.
[154] Kartar Lalvani, *The Making of India: The Untold Story of British Enterprise.* (London: Bloomsbury Continuum, 2016), 13.
[155] Ibid., 14.
[156] Ibid.

The office of Secretary of State for India was a new one for Britain. The secretary's office was located in London, and the name of his department, the India Office.[157] The Sepoy Rebellion of 1857 had illustrated the horrors of widespread mutiny. As the British crown took over administration of the country, ratios were placed on the British Army which prevented the number of Indian soldiers to British from exceeding 3 to 1.[158] This proved difficult to enforce, as the expense of stationing and maintaining British troops overseas in these ratios was expensive.

The first Secretary of State for India in 1874, Robert Arthur Talbot Gascoyne-Cecil

---

[157] Percival Griffiths., 83.
[158] Pradeep P. Barua, Gentlemen of the Raj: The Indian Army Officer Corps, 1817-1949 (Westport, CT: Praeger, 2003), 3.

The debate over the long-term effects on the Raj continues today. Colonial India, it is said by critics, was little more than a storehouse of raw materials and a market for British goods and her world empire. Others argue that though there were long- and short-term problems with the Raj, the British should receive credit for some contributions to India's benefit. These include the establishment of law and order that led to greater domestic peace and the extensive civil administration system that allowed the country of 347 million to function. In its 1958 report on "The New India," the Planning Commission of the Indian government celebrated India's new found independence, but stopped short of critiquing their former colonial masters, claiming, "The British withdrew from India in a manner honorable to both sides and worthy of their own rich tradition of freedom, leaving a fund of goodwill and eagerness on the part of India to forgive and forget and to remember only the best of the past."[159] The "best," according to government officials, included a "strong administrative structure of the former Government," a highly trained and organized" Indian Civil Service, and "the judiciary and police system which had established both a mechanism and respect for law and order over the entire country."[160]

To rule such a massive country as India required an efficient administration and many bureaucrats to carry out the everyday work of governing. The Indian Civil Service, in its earliest form established in 1757, did just that. At first, the Indian Civil Service was dominated by Britons with only a few, narrowly selected Indians who had attended university in England and passed the Civil Service exams in London. Eventually, the Indian Civil Service became a home for aspiring classes of Indian professionals, who, after 1923, could take the Civil Service exam (though still in English) without leaving the country.[161] After passing the exam, however, ICS recruits spent time in Britain, taking classes and acquiring the "British social graces" necessary for service to the Crown.[162]

Members of the ICS had a remarkable amount of independence, charged with administering their assigned colonial areas with little interference or direct supervision after an initial period of training under a British officer. At only 25 or 30, a member of the service would carry out British policy, largely improvising their own responses to crisis or challenge, since communication was rare and difficult.[163] These young men, however, also carried out their role in a way that restored confidence in the fairness of the British, rejecting corrupt practices that had been in place under the East India Company, administering justice and settling disputes instead, while traveling a district on horseback.[164]

In *Anglo-Indian Attitudes*, Clive Dewey chronicles the life and work of two Britons who

---

[159] Planning Commission, Government of India, The New India: Progress through Democracy (New York: Macmillan, 1958), 15.
[160] Ibid.
[161] Ibid.
[162] Ibid., 10.
[163] Ibid., 11-12.
[164] Ibid., 13.

dedicated their lives to service in the Indian Civil Service. He begins his work acknowledging it would likely draw criticism from opponents of British colonialism as well as those who believe that the presence of the British benefitted India. Dewey rejects the adoption of either position as legitimate when making judgment of the actions of individuals, choosing to "accept the possibility that ideas driven by the process of intellectual discovery direct our action by invading our minds."[165]

Dewey argues that within the Indian Civil Service were many men, who because of their childhoods, education, training, and actions, had an impact on Indian society that would be foolish for historians to ignore. Since the numbers of years of service for an ICS officer was 35, such men had more than enough time to shape the culture and policy in the areas in which they worked, often ruling over 300,000 people on their own.[166] There was, however, a divide in the ICS, which meant it "veered between…assimilation and preservation…between westernizers who wanted to change Indian and orientalists who loved it…"[167]

By the time India became independent, the 980-strong officer corps had over 500 native officers, many of who continued to serve through their 35-year commitment and beyond. The British ICS left the country, but not without misgivings, as one said in 1946: You want us to leave India. We would leave very soon but one thing you must remember that you would not be able to maintain those vaulting standards of fairness, honesty, efficaciousness and diligence in administration, which we maintained because of the conspicuous role of the ICS and other services despite difficulties of governing and numerous odds faced by us. Time would come when many of you would remember us with tears in your eyes.[168]

Under the crown, particular industries continued to flourish, though the lives of India's poorest did not dramatically change. About 70% of Indians remained agricultural workers. Those who entered businesses, those who grew crops that could be exported, and educated professionals saw great improvement in their economic status.[169] During the Raj, trade in both opium and indigo greatly declined, and new products–such as cotton, jute, iron, and wheat–began to dominate. Though much of what Indians produced brought about profit through export, some of these industries actually blocked out British products, as we will see below.[170]

Before the 1850s, cotton produced in India was largely exported to Europe for spinning or weaving. What was spun in India was completely by hand. The first steam-powered cotton mill did not reach India until 1856. Indians within the industry soon realized that their greatest profits could be made not in shipping raw materials to Europe, where it was difficult to compete, but in

[165] Clive Dewey, *Anglo-Indian Attitudes: Mind of the Indian Civil Service.* (London: The Hambledon Press, 1993), viii.
[166] Ibid., 12.
[167] Ibid., 14.
[168] R.K. Kaushik, "The Men Who Ran the Raj." Hindustan Times. April 17, 2012.
[169] McLeod, 86.
[170] Ibid., 86-87.

spinning in the new factories being built in India. The strategy worked. By becoming a leader in mechanized spinning, India beat out British competition and became the major supplier of yarn to China and Japan, as well as leading with 68% of domestic consumption. The addition of power looms in the 1880s meant more of the production process was kept at home. By the early 20th century, cotton textile production had become India's most important industry.[171] Unlike many other industries remaining in British hands, the cotton industry became truly domestic and is the best example of laissez-faire capitalism, which was the operant policy in India after the 1858 transition.[172] Gandhi would later condemn this westernization of India and call for a return to hand-spinning, both as a form of protest and salvation for India.

---

[171] Ibid., 86.

[172] B. B. Misra, The Indian Middle Classes: Their Growth in Modern Times (London: Oxford University Press, 1961), 215.

Gandhi

Railroad construction in India had begun before the Raj in 1850, and the first train operated in 1853.[173] The milestone of passenger transport was marked with great celebration as the British expressed the hope that "a well-designed system of Railways, ably and prudently executed, would be the most powerful of all worldly instruments of the advancement of civilization in every respect."[174] By 1861, there were over 1500 miles of railroad track completed. This number would be well over 40,000 miles by the late 1950s.[175] In his study of economic improvements under the Raj, I.D. Derbyshire, who rejects what he calls the "immiserationist" interpretation of the Raj. He also argues that recent scholarship tends to support a "meliorist," or positive, view of British rule.[176] Derbyshire cites three factors in the improvement of Indian life and per capita income growth for the native population: a peaceful and well-administered government after 1857; the expansion of European markets for raw goods and easier access to these markets through technology; and the development of India's rail system.[177] The railways constructed in India brought many benefits, including commercial reliability. Rail helped to alleviate the effects of monsoon rains on trade prior to rail travel. Though weather affected trains, the flow of commerce was steadier during the days of land and river transport, and they could be shut down completely at times. River and land transport also faced challenges as a result of changes being wrought in India. Though riverboat carriage was the cheapest form of transport for goods, it was also "risky, seasonal…and excruciatingly slow."[178] These problems were exacerbated by the effects of canal building in India which lowered river levels and made transport of goods by river even more challenging in certain areas. Land transport via pack animals improved after the innovation of the bullock cart, but faced challenges similar to those of the riverboat.

---

[173] Ian Kerr., *Engines of Change: The Railroads that Made India.* (Westport, Connecticut: Praeger, 2007), 5.
[174] Ibid., 6.
[175] Ibid., 10.
[176] Derbyshire, I. D. "Economic Change and the Railways in North India, 1860-1914." *Modern Asian Studies* 21, no. 3 (1987): 522.
[177] Ibid., 523.
[178] Ibid., 526.

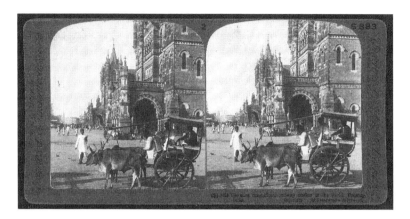

"The most magnificent railway station in the world." says the caption of the stereographic tourist picture of Victoria Terminus, Bombay, which was completed in 1888.

Railway construction would change the Indian economy radically and permanently, especially in Western India. Railways provided a vital link between India's fertile and heavily populated Doabs (regions of great agricultural yield due to rich soils and heavy cultivation) and the port cities of Bombay and Karachi.[179] Though Indian nationalist writers often claimed the changes wrought by rail were responsible for the famines that periodically struck India during the Raj, Derbyshire rejects their claim that agricultural production shifted from grains and subsistence farming to a singular focus on cash crops for exports such as sugar, indigo, and cotton. Instead, he claims rail and the accompanying lower shipping rates, as well as the opening of the Doabs to western ports, allowed production of both domestically consumed grains and cash crops to increase "in tandem."[180] Grain production, he states, actually increased, from 57,000 tons in the years between 1880-1884 to over 560,000 tons in the years prior to World War I. While some of the increase was shipped overseas to newly opened export markets, over 300,000 tons of grain during this period were shipped inward and consumed domestically.[181] Grain production was mixed with the production of crops that helped to restore the soil and allow for year-round production.

Rail also changed the traditional practices of Indian rural areas. It had been common practice for villages to build grain storage facilities and to store up the excess for protection against crop failures. While this storage had often saved lives in earlier times, the implementation of cheap rail transport made this type of grain storage obsolete. Grain could go immediately to market to meet the demand, and where disaster struck, rail allowed a targeted response. Comparing two

---

[179] Ibid., 527.
[180] Ibid., 530.
[181] Ibid.

periods of short supply, the 1860 crop failures (when rail access was still limited), saw famine conditions even with a transport of 175,000 tons of grain to affected areas. Similar conditions in 1907 were alleviated with 725,000 tons of grain shipped by rail.[182]

While Derbyshire's work rejects the overall claim that the rich grew richer and the poor grew poorer as a result of the Raj and rail, he concedes that the development of West Indian farming led to a decline for agricultural workers in the East. At the same time, he notes that rail benefitted eastern regions by creating cheap transportation opportunities for East Indian workers who found employment in the Jute mills.

The number of people who were transported by rail in India grew each year. In 1920, 175 million Indians traveled by train somewhere in the country.[183] The railroad also became one of the three largest employers of the Indian population, just behind the Indian Army, the post, and telegraph. Today, the railroad continues to employ 1.6 million Indians.[184]

British innovations, particularly in rail, Derbyshire claims, were not the direct cause of the negative impact nationalist writers often claim. While those critical of the Raj's impact would cite slowed population growth, famine, decreased native land holdings, and the decline of the handicraft industry as evidence, more recent scholarship indicates these problems were more localized and offset by gains in other areas. Though both sides would agree the more independent, middle-class farmers and upper classes benefitted much more and at a faster rate than the poorest agricultural workers, meliorists claim the negative impact of rail was the result of already existing poor hygiene which spread more quickly and easily as a result of rail transport. Derbyshire cites Gandhi on the matter, recalling his statement regarding "the protection of natural segregation was trenched upon and India was opened up to a scourge of disease such as South America had been in the 16th century."[185] He reminds his readers that cyclical famine as a result of crop failures was a part of Indian life, well before British rule, and in fact, that the impact of famine was greatly reduced post-1900 by the very existence of rail.

Of the four charges nationalist historians hold against the British, Derbyshire credits one: the decline of the handicraft industry. As far as the other charges, he exhorts the student of Indian history to consider the economic motives of the writers who were often the best-educated Indian natives, hailing from Bengal. It was, Derbyshire contends, the opening of prosperity to those in the lower classes and castes that influenced these writers to view the continuing changes as harmful. Having experienced the benefits of favorable relations with the British East India Company, they were loath to see opportunities open to all of India and not just to a select few. Additionally, Derbyshire calls his readers' attention to the conditions under which critical

---

[182] Ibid., 532.
[183] Ritika Prasad., *Tracks of Change: Railways and Everyday Life in Colonial India.* (Daryaganj: Cambridge University Press, 2015) 2.
[184] Kartar Lalvani, 21.
[185] Derbyshire., 539.

writing was undertaken, pointing out that during times of famine (in works he calls "gloomy"), the conclusions of nationalists were far more condemning of the British than during times of prosperity.[186]

In the final assessment of the benefits of British rail and accompanying economic change during the Raj, Derbyshire insists the division between those who condemn the Raj as negative and those who believe it benefitted India, results primarily, not from a difference in the data considered, but in the question asked. For nationalists, the question is: "Why did India not achieve takeoff?" asked in light of "their disappointment with comparative growth and income trends between India and Europe." For "meliorists," the question is instead: "Did per capita income rise between 1860 and 1920?"[187] He suggests that a middle ground, recognizing both significant growth and the limitations of that growth compared to other parts of the world, provides the most accurate accounting.[188]

Women and the Raj

In the wake of modern innovations and easier transport, British women began arriving in India in high numbers. The interaction between British women and the Indian people was largely relegated to inside British bungalows, removed from the crowded and busy living conditions of the Indians in Bombay, Calcutta, and Madras.[189] British ladies who often came to India to accompany their military husbands were called masters' women, or memsahibs.[190]

Margaret Macmillan's work on the lives of the women of the British Raj provides great insight as to their role in keeping British culture alive in the midst of a foreign and sometimes intimidating land. Though Macmillan often critiques British women for their lack of knowledge of the language, their assumption of superiority, and for "the greatest of all their incivilities...simply ignor[ing] India,"[191] she does not allow the modern perspective to prevent her from telling the story of the Raj. Instead, she cautions "to bundle them all up...into the stock figure of memsahib is to do to them what they did to the Indians."[192]

Certainly, life in India was far different than it would have been for the typical British woman. Whereas at home, most of the women would have been decidedly middle class, as representatives of the great British empire, they were expected to entertain and to take part in the "pomp and gaudy pageantry"[193] the Indians were taught to expect. To entertain at the expected level, the average British household in India might have 16 servants, each with specific tasks to

---

[186] Ibid., 543.
[187] Ibid., 544.
[188] Ibid.
[189] Margaret Macmillan, Women of the Raj: The Mothers, Wives, and Daughters of the British Empire in India. (New York: Random House Trade Books, 2007) 23.
[190] Ibid., xi.
[191] Ibid., xii.
[192] Ibid., 12.
[193] Ibid., xxii.

carry out.

British women in India were used to living with an ever-present fear of mutiny. The history of the Sepoy Rebellion and simple recognition of the ratio of British to Indians made the fears real. As one woman wrote, "I honestly confess that the overwhelming crowds of people frightened me…What were we in the land, I thought, but a handful of Europeans at best, and what was to prevent these myriads from falling upon and obliterating us, as if we never existed?"[194]

Though British women had legitimate fears living in India, they faced little of the daily struggles the majority of Indian women met feeding their families, protecting them from disease, and navigating the changing face of Indian culture.

That changes to the suttee (the practice of immolating oneself after the death of a husband), the remarriage of widows, polygamy, and the general status of women both inside and outside the home wrought under British rule cannot be disputed.[195] The reason for these changes is still under debate by historians. The traditional view held that British changes to the law—outlawing suttee, legalizing and promoting second marriages for Indian widows, and the British education of women–were largely responsible for the change. Some modern historians claim that the changes in women's roles were driven by upper-middle class Indians who aspired to the British way of doing things, "attributing the changes to a desire to emulate Victorian moral codes and aping a bourgeois form of companionate marriage."[196]

In fact, early British colonial policy in India instructed British courts to apply family law differently than in the rest of the legal code. Specifically, because of unfamiliar and centuries-long practices, such as infant and child marriage, British authorities in India were instructed to apply Hindu law to Hindu family disputes and Muslim law to Muslims. Early on, the concerns of the British East India Company were economic, and they opposed interventions they believed would negatively affect their profits. This was one of the reasons the Company opposed the entrance of Christian missionaries to India–something they were able to prevent until 1813, when the Company's charter was up for renewal.[197] It was only over time that the British changed their approach and began to directly intervene through legislation and practices designed to change the status and state of Indian women.[198]

British statesmen were convinced of the evils of Hinduism, calling it "the most enormous and tormenting suspicion that ever harassed and degraded any portion of mankind."[199] William Wilberforce and others considered introducing missionary efforts and Christian morals one the

---

[194] Ibid., 23.
[195] Ibid.
[196] Ibid.
[197] John Keay, 428.
[198] Domenico Francavilla,. "Interacting Legal Orders and Child Marriages in India." American University Journal of Gender Social Policy and Law 19, no. 2 (2011): 535-538.
[199] John Key, 428.

"greatest of all causes."[200] Gradually, the legal age of marriage was raised from ten in 1860 to twelve in 1891. The Hindu and Muslim populations resisted these changes, disputing the colonizers rights to intervene in private and religious matters, which were areas that had traditionally been left to Indians to regulate themselves. Rather than fight the legalities, the British chose to restrain the practices they believed were wrong than outlaw them completely. In 1929, the Marriage Restraint Act set criminal penalties for child marriages where the girl was under 12 or the boy under fifteen years of age.[201] John Keay takes a highly skeptical view of the reformers' motives and is critical of British attempts to eliminate customs such as suttee, which he claims were practiced rarely and not particularly linked to the Hindu faith.[202] He contends that with the introduction of the Christian mission, the British "became increasingly imbued with a sense of divine mission, their earlier toleration and even support of Indian religions evaporated, their conviction of Christianity's moral superiority grew, and their solicitude for the taboos of their subjects was eroded by carelessness and ignorance."[203]

The word, suttee, is, in fact, an English term used to describe the tradition in which an Indian wife would be burned to death in honor of her husband upon his funeral pyre. If a woman were pregnant at the time of her husband's death, or she was informed of his death after his body was disposed of–such as during wartime–the widow would be burned separately, with some personal item of his clothing as a symbol of his presence.[204] The Indian word *sati*, or faithful, was the word used to describe the widow herself, not the practice, the origin of which is disputed even by modern historians.[205]

The suttee appears to have been submitted to–and even desired–by many Indian widows. Was this due to pure religious belief and in honor of the gods, because of tradition, or perhaps, as Percival Griffiths suggests, a way to avoid the life that Indian widows–who were prevented by law and tradition from remarrying–were destined? Griffiths contends that "the life of a Hindu widow was one of misery. She was expected to eat only one meal a day, never to sleep on a bed, never to wear attractive clothes, and indeed to enter on a life of renunciation...friends and relatives next join together in lamenting her widowhood, and finally make her sit on a small stool. Then, one of her nearest female relatives, having previously muttered some religious formulae, cuts the thread of the tali, the gold ornament which every married woman in India wears round her neck. The barber is called in, and her head is clean shaved. This double ceremony sinks her instantly into the despised and hated class of widows...Doomed to perpetual widowhood, cast out of society, stamped with the seal of contumely, she has no consolation whatever except maybe the recollection of hardships she has had to endure during her married

[200] Ibid.
[201] Domenico Francavilla.
[202] John Keay, 429.
[203] Ibid.
[204] Edward Thompson, Suttee: A Historical and Philosophical Enquiry into the Hindu Rite of Widow Burning. (London: George Allan and Unwin Ltd., 1928), 15.
[205] Ibid.

life."[206]

Despite this, some Indians, and the majority of the British, opposed the practice of suttee, which was finally banned in Bengal, Calcutta, and Madras in 1829 and 1830, while India was still under the control of the East India Company. During this period, the Liberal party had taken control of the British government, and their perspective on the mother country's role in her colonies changed policy significantly.[207] The governor-general who banned the practice, Lord William Bentinck, attempted to use pressure and reward to promote the end of suttee throughout all of India, including those lands still controlled by Indian rulers. The practice itself was largely ended by 1850.[208]

Lord Bentinck

During the Raj, however, there were incidents of suttee reported by groups who desired to show their independence from the British or who wanted to return to the traditional ways. An incident often referred to as 'The Last Suttee," may show just how much the practice had

---

[206] Percival Griffiths, The British Impact on India (London: MacDonald, 1952), 219.

[207] Rudolf Von Albertini and Albert Wirz, European Colonial Rule, 1880-1940: The Impact of the West on India, Southeast Asia, and Africa, trans. John G. Williamson (Westport, CT: Greenwood Press, 1982), 6.

[208] Ibid., 225.

changed as a result of British and Indian opposition by the 1860s. When Mahrana Surup Singh died, a call was made to his multiple wives to become sati in his honor. The stakes were especially high, it was said, since the particular tribe in question had never had a leader cremated without a faithful wife to follow him into the next life. None of the wives agreed to participate, however, and instead, a young servant girl was compelled by her brother to receive the "honor." The child, like many who "willingly" participated in suttee, was put under much psychological pressure by both family members and the crowds who came to see the ceremony, and was given drugs that would render her state less than rational.[209] It should be noted that "every wife had, for the first time in the annals of Mewar, declined to die on such an occasion."[210]

Rudyard Kipling's famous poem, "The Last Suttee," was said to be based upon this incident, but in his romanticized version, the queen herself, disguised as "a North-bred dancing-girl," and too afraid of the fiery death of the pyre, asks her "brother" to kill her with the sword. Kipling records his version of events in the last moments of the suttee:

> He drew and struck: the straight blade drank
> The life beneath the breast.
> "I had looked for the Queen to face the flame,
> But the harlot dies for the Rajpoot dame–
> Sister of mine, pass, free from shame,
> Pass with thy King to rest!"
>
> The black log crashed above the white:
> The little flames and lean,
> Red as slaughter and blue as steel,
> That whistled and fluttered from head to heel,
> Leaped up anew, for they found their meal
> On the heart of–the Boondi Queen![211]

After 1858, suttee was rarely practiced, and often used as a show of defiance to English rule in pockets of resistance and tradition, though Edward Thompson, writing in 1928, insisted that "it would be easy to show that suttee, in one form or another, public or private and irregular, has occurred almost every year in some part of India between 1829 and 1913; and it probably will still occur, though at longer intervals."

---

[209] Edward Thompson, 112-113.

[210] Ibid., 113.

[211] Rudyard Kipling, *The Collected Poems of Rudyard Kipling*. (Hertfordshire: Wordsworth Editions Limited, 2004),248-251.

The University of Lucknow, founded by the British in India

Why the moral concern for India? Were British attempts at reform in such matters really just another for and of subjugation? To answer the question in full, one must examine the period before the Raj, when the foundation for education of the Indian people was being laid.

In 1819, Lord Hastings wrote that there would be a "time not very remote when England will wish to relinquish the domination which she has gradually and unintentionally assumed over this country, and from which she cannot at present recede."[212] For many British officials, there was a desire to see the Indian natives educated and the understanding that that education would eventually lead to self-rule. Though sounding paternalistic to the modern ear, another British official wrote of the ultimate goal for India to achieve self-rule: "We should look upon India, not as a temporary possession, but as one which is to be maintained permanently until the natives shall in some future age have abandoned most of their superstitions and prejudices, and become sufficiently enlightened, to frame a regular government for themselves, and to conduct and preserve it. Whenever such a time shall arrive, it will probably be best for both countries that the British control over India should be gradually withdrawn. That the desirable change contemplated may in some after-age be effected in India, there is no cause to despair. Such a

---

[212] Percival Griffiths, The British Impact on India (London: MacDonald, 1952), 245.

change was at one time in Britain itself at least as hopeless as it is here. When we reflect how much the character of nations has always been influenced by that of governments, and that some, once the most cultivated, have sunk into barbarism, while others, formerly the rudest, have attained the highest point of civilization, we shall see no reason to doubt that if we pursue steadily the proper measures, we shall in time so far improve the character of our Indian subjects as to enable them to govern and protect themselves."[213]

The effects of a classical Western education, it was understood, would necessarily lead to Indian independence. For some British leaders, any other result was unthinkable. This was true, not only in the decision to educate the Indian people, but in the debate about whether or not Indian natives should be allowed to hold high offices in the British administration. "Are we to keep these men submissive? or do we think we can give them knowledge without awakening ambition? or do we mean to awake ambition and provide it with no legitimate vent? Who will answer any one of these questions in the affirmative? Yet one of them must be answered in the affirmative by every person who maintains that we ought permanently to exclude the people of India from high office. I have no fears. The path of duty is plainly before us, and it is also the path of wisdom, of national prosperity, and of honour."[214]

As a 26-year-servant of the Indian Civil Service, Romesh Dutt found it "ungracious" and "painful" to criticize British policy, but found a sound basis for doing so in the very education provided to him in the mother country. Dutt quoted John Stuart Mill to support his charge that the very idea Britain would rule India in an unselfish manner was insupportable: "The government of a people by itself has a meaning and a reality; but such a thing as government of one people by another does not, and cannot exist. One people may keep another for its own use, a place to make money in, a human cattle-farm to be worked for the profits of its own inhabitants."[215]

Lord Macaulay debated the direction of British education in 1835 before the British Parliament. He acknowledged the debate between those who believed the future of education should be conducted in the native languages of India (the Orientalists) and those who believed that English must become the official language of the empire (the Anglicizers), but sided with those that advocated English, believing that "it is impossible for us, with our limited means, to attempt to educate the body of the people. We must at present do our best to form a class who may be interpreters between us and the millions whom we govern, a class of persons Indian in blood and colour, but English in tastes, in opinions, in morals and in intellect. To that class we may leave it to refine the vernacular dialects of the country, to enrich those dialects with terms of science borrowed from the Western nomenclature, and to render them by degrees fit vehicles for

---

[213] Ibid., 246.
[214] Ibid., 247.
[215] Martin Deming Lewis, ed., Romesh Dutt. British in India: Imperialism or Trusteeship? (Boston: D.C. Heath, 1962). 5.

conveying knowledge to the great mass of the population."[216]

By the 1850s and after the rebellion in 1857, many leaders of the Raj opposed the idea of an education that would lead to independence.[217] Instead, they fought inclusion of natives in places of authority and believed that the education of Indians was wasteful at best, and likely dangerous. But as Percival Griffiths explains, by this time, the forces of Indian independence had already been planted and would come to fruition.[218] Whether or not the Brits of 1857 and beyond realized it, "India's new young leaders-in-embryo…learned from their early failures how better to appeal for justice, equality of opportunity, and fair play–British ideals they culled from the works of Milton, Macaulay, Mill, and Morley, which they memorized and articulated more eloquently than did most British officials."[219]

The debate over whether the education of the Indians would concentrate on Western literature and science, or be taught by Hindus and in Sanskrit, was overwhelmingly won by those who advocated the former as the best path for India to modernize. There were individuals and families, however, who continued to prize the learning of Sanskrit, the ancient language of the priesthood, even as most English-educated Indians were pursuing Latin.[220]

Many Indian families prized the idea of a Western education and sacrificed time, money, and effort in order to obtain one for their children, as "the conviction grew steadily stronger among literate families that English education was essential to future prosperity and status."[221] Though in the larger cities of Calcutta, Bombay, and Madras, obtaining an English education was a matter of only registering and paying, in more isolated areas of the country, or in areas where native rulers prevented the establishment of English schools, children often had to travel to school, and many left home and lived at English boarding schools in the large cities.

Despite the desire for a Western education, which most believed would greatly aid in the economic advantages for the family, some Indian families worried about their sons taking on Western ways of relating to family and family authority, rejection of Indian traditions, and their potential conversion to Christianity. Therefore, the missionary schools were sometimes avoided by conservative families who wanted to ensure there would be no pressure or influence to reject Hinduism or Islam.

For women, educational avenues were opened up by the British, even if modern historians

---

[216] Thomas B. Macaulay. Bureau of Education. Selections from Educational Records, Part I (1781-1839). Edited by H. Sharp. Calcutta: Superintendent, Government Printing, 1920. Reprint. Delhi: National Archives of India, 1965, 107-117.
[217] Percival Griffiths, 247.
[218] Ibid., 248.
[219] Stanley Wolpert, "A Mixed Legacy: From the Raj to Modern India," Harvard International Review 32, no. 4 (2011).
[220] Judith E. Walsh, Growing Up in British India: Indian Autobiographers on Childhood and Education under the Raj (New York: Holmes & Meier, 1983), 36.
[221] Ibid., 38.

"have been more critical of the gender perspective of these liberal reformers, attributing the changes to a desire to emulate Victorian moral codes and aping a bourgeois form of companionate marriage."[222] The reasons behind the desire to educate young Indian women may be many, but the results,–the elimination of the suttee, laws against the remarriage of widows, and female infanticide[223]–surely improved the lives of Indian women despite the motives of those calling for female education and reform.

In 1906, the new Secretary of State for India, John Morley, met with Indian Muslims. He "was planning the most far-reaching constitutional changes that India had seen since 1858,"[224] reforms that included separate elections for Muslims in India and the platform for the creation of the All-India Muslim League.[225] Morley was an idealist, who, though he stopped short of believing that India should rule herself, had the desire to see many more Indians from the middle class taking part in her governance.[226] After meeting with Indian nationalists in London in 1906, Morley wrote to the Earl of Minto, India's Viceroy, saying, "Not one more whit than you do I think it desirable or possible, or even conceivable, to adapt English political institutions to the nations who inhabit India. Assuredly not in your day or mine. But the spirit of English institutions is a different thing, and it is a thing that we cannot escape even if we wished."[227]

---

[222] Tanika Sarkar, "Women in South Asia: The Raj and After," History Today, September 1997.
[223] Ibid.
[224] John McLeod, 98.
[225] Ibid.
[226] Colin Cross, The Liberals in Power, 1905-1914 (London: Barrie and Rockliff, 1963), 50.
[227] Ibid., 51.

Morley

Minto

What would become known as the Morley-Minto reforms had two aspects, the administrative and legislative, both of which operated on the underlying principle of including more Indians in governmental decision-making. To that end, the viceroy named an Indian to his cabinet for the first time, and Morley named two Indians to the London council.[228]

The fight for the rights of Indians would dominate the next 40 years of Anglo-Indian relations. One of the key aspects of the debate was whether Indians should seek to gain rights as a single and unified political entity, or whether the various groups in India (Hindus, Mulims, Sikhs, etc.) should seek to carve out rights for themselves by dealing directly with the British. Legislatively, Morley promised the Muslims voting rights, but his critics claimed that Morley's reforms "were so full of the idea of Communal elections that 'the very thought of India vanished from the Bill, to be replaced by consideration for the separate communities of Hindu, Mohammedan, Sikh, Mahratta, non-Brahmin, Indian Christian, Anglo-Indian and English'—that is to say, representatives to the Assemblies and elsewhere were to be elected, not as Indians, but as Hindus, Mohammedans, Sikhs, Christians, etc.; and not to serve India, their common country, but to serve primarily their own particular classes and religious sects."[229]

Morley's critics saw his reaching out to the Muslim minorities, not as a move toward equality

---

[228] Ibid.
[229] Jabez T. Sunderland, India in Bondage (New York: Lewis Copeland Company, 1932), 238.

of reform, but as a way to continue to divide the Indian people. Morley-Minto ensured, one critic said, that there would be no actual progress made for Indian self-government, at least for another decade.[230] Other critics saw the reforms as a minimal response to the inevitable development of Indian independence. These critics emphasize the growing influence of India's educated professional class and over 60 million Muslims, both of which represented a growing challenge to Britain's rule. Cynical about the motives behind the reforms, they claim Morley and Minto "were consistent with the governing principle of the Indian prince who consulted his notables in durbar while reserving his autocracy,"[231] citing WWI, not British political reforms, as the real harbinger of independence.[232]

Critiques of the Raj and the End of It

For all the accomplishments of the Raj, many British and Indians alike offered criticism of the British policy in India. This critique did not always accuse the British of bringing no improvements to India, but instead, pointed out that the benefits that did come with the East India Company, and later with direct rule, were beneficial primarily to Westerners. In the short-term, many local artisans and craftspeople were put out of business, but in the long term, critics said, the harm was far more devastating, resulting in long-term poverty and destructive patterns.

Romesh Dutt, a Calcutta-born 26-year member of the Indian Civil Service, was educated in the West. Like so many exposed to a Western education, he eventually critiqued the very system that had employed him, and resigned his position to become a voice for Indian independence.[233] He commended the British for their contributions, which he lists as peace, Western education, a strong administrative government, and a pure justice system,[234] calling these "results which no honest critic of British rule in India regards without high admiration."[235] Nevertheless, Dutt offers much critique for Britain's economic approach in India, arguing, "it is, unfortunately, true that the East India Company and the British Parliament, following the selfish commercial policy of a hundred years ago, discouraged Indian manufacturers in the early years of British rule in order to encourage the rising manufactures of England."[236] Dutt criticizes the British in three areas: their trade policies–which "crippled" India's manufacturing; their impressive, yet devastating, collection of a land tax; and their demand for interest on the debt owed by India to the mother country as a result of the 1857 rebellion.[237]

Another Indian writer, Kartar Lalvani, has written a book that seeks to defend Britain's record

---

[230] Ibid., 239.
[231] William Roger Louis, Andrew Porter, and Alaine M. Low, eds., The Oxford History of the British Empire, vol. 3 (Oxford: Oxford University Press, 1999), 444.
[232] Ibid., 444-5,
[233] Romett Dutt in Martin Deming Lewis, 1.
[234] Ibid.
[235] Ibid.
[236] Ibid., 2.
[237] Ibid., 5.

in India. As a 50-year resident of England, Lalvani claims to have been unable to find a single Brit who would name a positive aspect of the British governance of India. Without denying that Britain was guilty–as many other nations have been–of exploiting India for her wealth, Lalvani's perspective is that once the country passed out of the hands of the British East India company and directly to the Crown, the contributions were positive and should be judged fairly.[238] He states, "The indisputable fact is that India, as a nation as it stands today, was originally created by a small, isolated island nation. India has endured as a democracy and as a unified nation thanks to the all-important and fully functional infrastructure of an independent civil service and judiciary, a disciplined and apolitical army and a well-drilled and efficient police force, all developed by the imperial power. Of course, the labor was local, indeed skillful, and the indigenous cultures were ancient and sophisticated, but it is worth pausing to consider what India would be like today if the British had chosen to stay at home."[239]

Author of *Indian Tales of the Raj*, Zareer Masani, describes his encounters with those who had lived through the British occupation period. Many of them bristle at what they saw as the British "obsession" with the Raj period, believing that other periods and influences are a more significant story for modern India. Thankfully, Masani pressed forward to record the remembrances of those who had lived through the period, whether highly critical of the British administration, cooperative, or in strong support.[240]

In 1885, only four years before the birth of Jawaharlal Nehru, the Indian National Congress organized and began the path to Indian independence. Still in its infant stages, the Congress would not see its goal complete until 1947. The Congress and the young man who would come to dominate it endured a long journey, fraught with delays and opposition, until he became India's first independent prime minister.

In its early stages, the Congress acted as a training ground for India's newly educated and politically awakened young men to hone their leadership skills. Meeting initially during the Christmas season, they passed a series of resolutions for change in India's governance, demanding "greater access by Indians to positions of governmental power, fewer taxes, reductions in military expenditure, and compulsory elementary education."[241] Although the resolutions coming out of the Congress were often ignored by British officials, "India's new young leaders-in-embryo…learned from their early failures how better to appeal for justice, equality of opportunity, and fair play–British ideals they culled from the works of Milton, Macaulay, Mill, and Morley, which they memorized and articulated more eloquently than most

---

[238] John Preston, "The British Were Imperialist Brutes? No, Britain Made India Great (says an Indian)". UK Daily Mail, 17 March 2016.

[239] Kartar Lalvani, *The Making of India: The Untold Story of British Enterprise*. (London: Bloomsbury Continuum, 2016), 2.

[240] Zareer Masani, Indian Tales of the Raj. (Berkeley: University of California Press, 1987), 1-6.

[241] Stanley Wolpert, "A Mixed Legacy: From the Raj to Modern India," Harvard International Review 32, no. 4 (2011).

British officials."[242]

Jawaharlal Nehru was born into a well-off Indian family and educated at English boarding schools, where he received a classical education along with many of his contemporaries. While at Harrow, he was exposed to a biography of the Italian nationalist Garibaldi, a figure who captured his imagination and admiration.[243] His later admiration of the Irish Independence movement caused Nehru to come into conflict with his moderate father, who had put great stock in the Raj early on, and enjoyed the benefits of British favor.[244] His son, having graduated from Cambridge and studying to pass the barrister's exam, eventually embraced a similar lifestyle in London, despite his attraction to the more radical elements of the Indian independence movement and a growing resentment of discrimination, which he regularly experienced at University.[245]

Nehru

[242] Ibid.
[243] Benjamin Zachariah, Nehru (New York: Routledge, 2004), 17.
[244] Ibid., 21.
[245] Ibid., 27.

In 1912, upon his return to India to begin practicing law with his father, the Swadeshi movement was already well underway. Swadeshi, meaning "of our own country," encouraged the forsaking of British goods and the colonial lifestyle, a movement that Nehru's family rejected. Instead, his father purchased a British automobile, marking himself as a man interested in continued cooperation and loyalty to the British way of life, in the mind of his son. Nevertheless, Nehru remained a faithful son, marrying a Brahmin girl in a match arranged by his father.[246]

Nehru remained interested in Indian independence, and resented what he saw as the divide and conquer methods employed by the British—emphasizing the enmity between Muslim and Hindu populations and helping to form the Muslim League, which would fight for its own rights, rather than for the recognition of Indian rights as a whole. The 1916 Lucknow Pact, signed by both the Muslim League and the National Congress, brought Hindus and Muslims together, as well as helping to promote cooperation between the two opposing independence parties, one more radical, the other more moderate, in its demands for home rule.

It was there, at the Lucknow Conference, that Nehru first met Mahatma Gandhi. Gandhi had returned to India from South Africa in 1915, where he had campaigned for better treatment of Indian soldiers stationed there by the British.[247] After spending a year touring India, Gandhi began his non-cooperation movement, encouraging civil disobedience, specifically appealing to Indian peasants through his peasant dress and manner of speaking.[248] Nehru's biographer, Benjamin Zechariah, notes that at the time of their Lucknow meeting, Nehru was "unable...to relate to [Gandhi's} style."[249] Though Nehru's father had joined the independence movement (largely as a result of British persecution of those who called for it), the Nehrus believed the path to Indian independence lay in the hands of the upper-middle, educated class, not in embracing the cause of Indian peasants or support of the British during WWI.[250]

India supported the British and her victorious allies during WWI, sending 1.5 million soldiers to war, funded with Indian revenue. During the war, progress was made in domestic industry and many British exports were disrupted. These factors led many to believe that Britain would now take its promises regarding India's independence seriously. Despite some action–such as the Montagu-Chelmsford reforms, which moderates believed held hope for the future–many Indians believed that "the British were willing to leave India–but always tomorrow."[251] The British agreed to further training for Indian nationalists, but also claimed their immediate removal would lead to conflict between the Muslims and Hindus and a vacuum of power in the East that would destabilize the world.

[246] Ibid., 28.
[247] Ibid., 33.
[248] Stanley Wolpert.
[249] Zechariah, 33.
[250] Ibid., 33-4.
[251] Ibid., 35.

Along with reform and cooperation, the British became increasingly dedicated to putting down the radicals who demanded a timetable they were unwilling to give. This was to be accomplished, in part, by extending the Rowlatt Bills, allowing martial law in India during the war.

Gandhi responded by launching his first Indian Satyagraha,[252] a tactic he had used successfully in South Africa. The movement encouraged Indians to "court arrest,"[253] an idea Nehru also embraced, though his father did not. Father and son would be divided in their agreement over the tactics employed in pursuing justice for India. Gandhi's methods, in fact, continued to confuse the more established independence movement. The head of the Muslim League, Muhammad Ali Jinnah, also protested the Rowlatt Bills, but both the Muslims and Hindus in Congress believed "Gandhi's 'extreme program' attracted the inexperienced and the illiterate, and caused further division everywhere in the country."[254]

Gandhi called for a rejection of British custom, including the burning of all British clothing, a boycott of British goods, and the unity of Muslims and Hindus in the fight to repeal the Rowlatt laws. He advised his followers to conduct their protest openly and without resistance to arrest, believing the appeal to right and justice, rather than violence, would win the day. Gandhi's methods were considered both dangerous and offensive by many British officials, including Winston Churchill, who believed that any willingness on the part of the British government to negotiate with Gandhi would be interpreted as weakness. Churchill was offended by what he believed was a deliberate deception by the man he referred to as a "seditious middle Temple lawyer"[255] to engage the support of the Indian people against British rule: "Gandhi, with deep knowledge of the Indian peoples, by the dress he wore—or did not wear, by the way in which his food was brought to him at the Vice regal Palace, deliberately insulted, in a manner which he knew everyone in India would appreciate, the majesty of the King's representative. These are not trifles in the East. Thereby our power to maintain peace and order among the immense masses of India has been sensibly impaired."[256]

---

[252] Stanley Wolpert, Gandhi's Passion: The Life and Legacy of Mahatma Gandhi (New York: Oxford University Press, 2002), 99.
[253] Zechariah, 36.
[254] Wolpert, Gandhi's passion, 100.
[255] Ramachandra Guha, "Churchill and Gandhi", The Hindu Magazine. June 19, 2005.
[256] Ibid.

Churchill in the early 20th century

Gandhi's April 1919 arrest led to heightened tensions in India as violence broke out in response. Though Gandhi rejected the violence on his behalf as a violation of satyagraha, the British continued to see resistance to the Rowlatt laws and developed a growing fear of Indian revolt.

On April 13, in one of the biggest turning points in India's history, a gathering of unarmed celebrants at Amritsar, or Jallianwala Bagh, was fired upon by British soldiers under the command of Reginald Dyer. Over 400 were killed.[257] As the details of the massacre were

---

[257] Stanley Wolpert, Gandhi's Passion, 101.

discovered (initially Gandhi himself blamed the Punjabis and tended to believe the British were in the right), the event "effectively killed moderate opinion in India."[258]

Gandhi in 1919

Throughout the 1920s, as the non-cooperation movement gained strength and popularity thus endangering the status quo, Nehru, his father, and Gandhi were all in and out of jail. Gandhi, whether jailed or free, continued to be the force behind the movement which ebbed and flowed with his words. For example, when a protest grew out of hand and a building was burned to the ground with British police inside in 1922, Gandhi suspended the movement, stating that if independence came by violence, it proved the Indian people were not ready to deserve it.[259]

---

[258] Zachariah, 38.
[259] Ibid., 47-49.

Nehru turned to socialism as the liberating force for India, while Gandhi retreated to semi-seclusion to restore himself both physically and spiritually. Frustrated and angry at the delay in progress, Nehru angrily wrote to Gandhi: "What then can be done? You say nothing—you only criticize and no helpful lead comes from you."[260] Nehru's ultimate rejection of the non-violence movement and full conversion to communism was soon to come. Gandhi's biographer explains: "To hold such an idealist as young Nehru in check Gandhi knew that he would have to abandon his life of rural retreat, returning first to the hurly-burly of urban political chaos like that he had found so hateful in Calcutta, and then to the enforced solitude of long years behind British bars and barbed wire walls."[261]

Nehru had no faith in hand spinning, or the return to simpler and less Western times Gandhi advocated. He also considered Gandhi's ancient Hindu ideals outdated and impractical, if not reactionary. But by the end of the decade, Gandhi emerged once again, hoping to save India from Nehru's now-communist leanings (despite their sometimes strained friendship) and accomplish independence in both a political and spiritual sense.

The Hindu-Muslim Divide

"Long years ago, we made a tryst with destiny and now the time comes when we shall redeem our pledge." – Jawaharlal Nehru

The origins of the Hindu-Muslim antipathy in India can be traced to the original entry of Muslim invaders into the sub-continent, and comparisons have often been made to the arrival of the Muslims in India and the later arrival of the British. Unlike earlier migrations of Aryans and Kushans, from whom were drawn the fundamental elements of Indian Hindu society, both the British and the various Muslim waves remained aloof and culturally exclusive. The British, of course, never claimed to be Indian and retained the advantage of a separate homeland, while the Muslims chose to integrate to the extent that they claimed the subcontinent as a homeland, but at the same time adopted a separate identity.

German diplomat Wilhelm von Pochhammer, who served extensively in India and wrote widely on Indian politics and history, made essentially this observation in his book *India's Road to Nationhood*, published first in 1981 and which remains today one of the most impartial and reliable accounts of the era. "The Central Asiatic Moslems," Pochhammer wrote, "who came to India had no homeland. They were forced to look upon conquered land as their new homeland, although each day showed them that for the mass of the subjugated people they remained foreigners."

The Muslims — if such an observation were to be accepted, and it is certainly not by any means universally accepted — played the role of a governing aristocracy, aloof from the masses

---

[260] Stanley Wolpert, *Gandhi's Passion.*, 129.
[261] Wolpert, 133.

and separated by their religious exclusivity and their foreign origins. They were never absolute aliens, like the British, but they were never Indians. They were also driven by the missionary zeal, so common among Abrahamic religions, to convert the masses to their own faith, and such an attitude immediately implies an imperviousness to any reciprocating adaption. History, of course, would prove that India's Islamic invaders failed to convert the mass of Hindus to Islam, achieving at the very best an accommodation within India for a Muslim minority.

With the arrival of the British, however, power was gradually transferred from Muslim to Anglo/Christian hands. Initially, therefore, the Muslim ruling elite resented the gradual British takeover, while it was generally embraced by the Hindus, for whom it meant liberation from Muslim domination. To India, Britain introduced Western education and modernization, which tended to favor the development of Hindu elites more than Muslim. The concept of the "Indian Renaissance" is generally understood to have come about thanks to these influences. Indian reformer and revivalist Raja Rammohan Roy was one of the earliest propagators of modern Western education, seeing it as a powerful instrument for the spread of modern ideas in India. He was associated with the foundation the Hindu College in Calcutta (which later came to be known as the Presidency College). He also maintained at his own cost an English school in Calcutta and, in addition, established Vedanta College, where both Indian learning and courses in Western social and physical science were offered.

That is not to say that Muslim leaders did not recognize a need to compete in this regard. One such was Syed Ahmad bin Muttaqi Khan KCSI, more commonly known as Sir Syed. Syed Khan was an Indian Muslim "pragmatist", Islamic reformist, and philosopher of nineteenth-century British India. He too recognized the advantageous elements of British rule, establishing such prestigious institutions as the Mohamedan Anglo-Oriental College, founded in 1875, which later emerged as Aligarh Muslim University.

This institution in due course became the seedbed of the parallel "Muslim Renaissance", which refused to ally itself with the "Indian Renaissance" insofar as it was dominated by Hindus, urging instead a wider embrace and appreciation of Islam. He went on to found the Muslim Educational Council, the Indian Patriotic Association, and the Mohammedan Defense Association of Upper India. Clearly, Sir Syed, alongside his reform agenda, championed the notion of a separate Muslim identity.

The 1858 arrival of Imperial Britain in India, while igniting this parallel movement, was also quick to recognize the potential of playing one off against the other to its own advantage. This, a tried and tested British imperial strategy, aided each individual community's march toward modernity, while at the same time stirring up the latent residue of their mutual loathing.

The Muslim portion of the Bengali population generally welcomed the partition of the territory into east and west, recognizing the immediate precedent that this established for separate territorial cantons. Lord Curzon pleaded publicly that the move was strictly administrative, but even if this was so, the message that it sent was clear enough. The British were prepared to tolerate territorial separation, and so a two-state solution was feasible.

This tacit approval was soon afterward codified into law with a series of constitutional reforms undertaken in 1909, known as the Morley-Minto Reforms. During the framing of these reforms, Sir Sultan Muhammed Shah, the Aga Khan, put pressure on the British government for a separate Muslim electorate, which was acknowledged and accepted and included in the Act of 1909. If Lord Curzon's partition of Bengal provided the precedent, the constitutional reforms of 1909 established that precedent in law. The extension of this to actually putting forward a geographic area as a potential Muslim state was achieved consequent to a second series of constitutional reforms under the chairmanship of Sir John Allsebrook Simon, who arrived in British-occupied India in 1928. As Sir John Simon's took evidence, the League proposed the provinces of Sind and Baluchistan, both now a province of Pakistan, as separate Muslim territories. This proposition was not adopted by the commission, and no one really thought that it would, but names had nonetheless been mentioned and aspirations ventilated, and for the time being, that was enough.

It has often been remarked that India was created by the British, and certainly, it was the British that combined the multiple kingdoms and fiefdoms of the sub-continent into a single nation, and it was opposition to the continuation of British rule and a common determination of overthrow it that united that nation. At the same time, an unfortunate feature of Indian political development during the early 20th century was the inability of Congress (and the Indian nationalist movement in general) to attract the participation of the Muslim minority. For this, many reasons were offered, including the Islamic view of cow-killing, language exclusivities, a conspicuous Muslim alliance with the British, and perhaps even a movement among Muslims at the time. All of this suggested that Islam differed from Hinduism in its compatibility with Western values and thinking, and these explanations sought to account for a seemingly enduring and suppurating antipathy that had endured for centuries and which simply would not heal.

By the late 19th century, however, the longevity of this division had almost nothing to do with conventions of religion, education, or modern thinking, and everything to do with politics. At the root of it lay a Muslim fear of domination by Hindus, if the Hinducentric Congress sought to position itself as the sole representative of the nation. It was self-evident to the Muslim minority leadership that the Indian Muslim community, in general, could not hope to prevail under democratic rules quite as it had under the British, and thus exclusivity and communalism began increasingly to inform Muslim political rhetoric.

The British, meanwhile, exacerbated this resurgent hostility between Hindus and Muslims when the decision was made in 1905 to partition the eastern province of Bengal.[262] This was

---

[262] The Partition of Bengal divided the provincial state of Bengal into predominantly Hindu West Bengal and the predominantly Muslim East Bengal. East Bengal would form the basis of East Pakistan and later the independent state of Bangladesh.

ordered by the then Viceroy of India, Lord Curzon, ostensibly to improve administrative efficiency, but in practical terms, it was to separate Muslims and Hindus in a region of India where populations were somewhat even and where communal violence was commonplace and growing. Hindus, of course, saw this as an extension of the British divide-and-rule policy, which was not wholly untrue, while Muslims saw it as the first tacit acknowledgement by the British that separation was the only solution.

It was around this event that Muslim separatism first began to find expression. In the East Bengali capital of Dhaka, a year after partition, the All-India Muslim League was founded as the voice of the Muslim minority. Obviously, the time and location of this must be viewed in the context of the partition, and notwithstanding protestations to the contrary, the formation of the Muslim League was an unmistakable precursor to Muslim pleas for separation. Like Congress, the early political temper of the Muslim League, or simply the League, was moderate and conservative, but despite this, its mere formation sowed the seeds of communalism in the wider political discourse of India, setting the Muslim minority on a separate political course.

In the 1910s, Muhammad Ali Jinnah represented the Muslim facet of the Indian independence movement, and like Nehru and Gandhi, he was a British-trained lawyer.[263] He was Muslim, of a minority faction, and of comparatively humble background. He was a spare and aesthetic man, more generous in his opinion of the British, and generally, he stood apart from the likes of Gandhi and Nehru in his willingness to collaborate and cooperate. The minority status of Muslims in India tended to soften Muslim attitudes towards the British, insofar as it was under British, secular rule that the Muslims were protected from inevitable numerical domination by Hindus. Jinnah served on the Imperial Legislative Council and was a Congress member, but he stood somewhat in the "unity" camp. He was initially opposed to the formation of the All-India Muslim League, taking the position that any principle of separate electorates simply served to divide the nation.

---

[263] Nehru was significantly senior in both caste and professional attributes to both Gandhi and Jinnah. His secondary education was completed at Harrow, second only to Eton as the most prestigious British private school, from where he gained entry to Trinity College Cambridge, equally prestigious.

Jinnah and Gandhi

While remaining a member of Congress, Jinnah joined the Muslim League in 1913, although he continued to serve and stand as the principal Muslim voice in Congress. In 1916, however, he was elected to the presidency of the Muslim League, with now a foot in both camps, and in that capacity, he was instrumental in negotiating the terms of the Lucknow Pact. The Lucknow Pact was an important agreement between the two parties that undertook to increase pressure on the British for greater Indian representation and to establish quotas for Hindu and Muslim representation on the various councils and committees that were open to Indian participation.

During World War I, Jinnah stood on the "dominion" platform, which preceded the Purna Swaraj movement with the demand that India be granted the same dominion status as the white colonies. In this regard, he suffered the same general disillusion as other Indian nationalist leaders as they reeled under the effects of the Jallianwala Bagh Massacre after World War I. Like many Muslims, he was depressed by the collapse of the Ottoman Empire and the disempowerment of the Ottoman caliphate. It all tended to compound a sense in his mind that the tide of history was tipping away from Indian Muslims and toward Indian Hindus.

As a lawyer and a constitutionalist, Jinnah instinctively opposed Gandhi, disturbed by the extra-constitutional nature of non-cooperation and satyagraha. His relationship with Gandhi (and vice versa) would always be chilly and restrained, and the two never managed to muster any real affection for one another. He remained publicly cordial toward Gandhi, however, no doubt recognizing the folly of swimming against a tide of popular adoration for the Mahatma among both impoverished Hindus and Muslims.

After the war, Jinnah sought to distance himself from both Congress and the League. He resigned from Congress and passed most of the 1920s away from the center of the Indian political stage. In his absence, the independence movement continued to gather momentum, quite as British opposition to it continued to solidify. Winston Churchill, always an influential voice of the British conservative movement, bitterly opposed any suggestion of Indian independence, and his personal antipathy toward Gandhi found expression in his usual acerbic wit, for which he has since become universally famous. The "half-naked fakir," Churchill opined, "ought best to be bound hand and foot and crushed by an elephant ridden by the viceroy."[264]

The essence of Churchill's opposition to Indian independence or any move toward it was the impoverishment within Britain that would follow the removal of India from the British economic equation. The 1929 British general election, however, removed the Conservative government of Stanley Baldwin from office, and it also removed Winston Churchill from the cabinet office of Chancellor of the Exchequer. The government was replaced with the Labor administration of Ramsay MacDonald. The MacDonald administration, by definition more liberal than the previous Conservative government, was nonetheless influenced by the same general forces. Various round table conferences and fact-finding missions sought in vain to find that elusive formula that would satisfy Indian nationalist fervor and at the same time require Britain to relinquish no actual political control.

Meanwhile, the 1930s dawned, and an increasingly defiant and maturing Congress raised the tricolor flag of independent India on the banks of the Ravi River in Lahore, defining the future direction of the movement. A month later, on January 26, 1930, Congress issued a declaration of sovereignty and self-rule, or Purna Swaraj, implicit in which was a stated readiness to withhold taxes as part of a revival of Gandhi's campaign of civil disobedience.

A Congress working committee then authorized Gandhi to put this declaration into effect by organizing the first orchestrated, Congress-sanctioned act of civil disobedience. Gandhi, as was his habit, meditated deeply on this. The most obvious and generally deplored British tax then in effect was the 1882 Salt Tax, which underwrote an official government monopoly on salt production by banning the traditional, communal production of salt. Violation of the Salt Act was a criminal offense, and Gandhi chose a mass violation of the British salt laws as the vehicle for his national satyagraha.

---

[264] The context of this comment was a meeting of the West Essex Conservative Association, specially convened so that Churchill could explain his position. He remarked: "…It is alarming and also nauseating to see Mr Gandhi, a seditious Middle Temple lawyer, now posing as a fakir of a type well known in the East, striding half-naked up the steps of the Vice-regal palace … to parley on equal terms with the representative of the King-Emperor.'

Initially, neither Congress nor the British took the notion of passive resistance centered on salt particularly seriously, but as a point of issue, it satisfied Gandhi's typical preference for simplicity, as well as touching to the heart of the petty and mean-spirited nature of British monopolistic legislation. Indians were legally disallowed from utilizing the universal resource of the sea to produce salt and were instead required to purchase it, contributing thus a tax revenue that affected the poorest Indians most acutely.

It took very little to stoke popular outrage, and Gandhi, with his flair for the theatrical and a very shrewd history of using the popular press, began to do just that. He added to a building anticipation in the countryside by issuing regular declamations against the British, and his public meditations and performances proved emotive and enormously influential. His satyagraha would take the form of a march.

The concept of a "march" had been accidentally arrived at in South Africa, during a series of Indian labor strikes and had proved in practice to be wildly successful. It had popular appeal and held the potential to gather momentum over an extended period. Gandhi set off from his Sabarmati Ashram in rural Gujarat on March 12, 1930 at the head of a small entourage of followers, intending to walk the 240 miles to the coastal village of Dandi in order to symbolically contravene the law by producing a small amount of salt.

By the time he reached Dandi and boiled a pot of seawater, he was surrounded by an entourage of some 50,000 people. This number, however, was dwarfed by the subsequent mass civil disobedience movement that swept the country. Millions broke the salt laws by manufacturing or purchasing illegal salt. British cloth and numerous other manufactured goods were boycotted, and many similar laws were overtly broken. Some 60,000 arrests were made. Violence broke out in a great many places, but this time Gandhi, aside from appealing for an end to it, did not suspend the action. Several sub-marches were mounted, one by a Muslim Pashto disciple of Gandhi, Ghaffar Khan, in the province of Peshwar, which resulted in troops firing on protesters, killing upward of 200. Indeed, a platoon of the Royal Garhwal Rifles refused, in the end, orders to fire on the crowd.

It was an unprecedented event on a national scale that shook the British administration to its core. Gandhi was arrested, and without charge or trial, he was jailed. Nine months later, however, fearing a popular reaction, he was released unconditionally, and soon afterward, what was known as the Gandhi-Irwin Pact (Lord Irwin was then Viceroy of India) was signed. This essentially committed the British government to negotiate a path toward self-government, and the result of this was the Government of India Act of 1935, a partial roadmap to Indian independence. Although the act committed the British government to make many authentic concessions to Indian demands, it nonetheless fell short of an actual grant of independence.

Despite this, it was a huge step in the right direction, including the grant of limited franchise to millions of Indians. The three major provisions, however, included the establishment of a loose federal structure, achieving a degree of provincial autonomy, and safeguarding minority interests through separate electorates.

In 1937, the act came into effect, although without its federal provisions, thanks primarily to opposition from rulers of the Princely States. An election, however, was held that, although of limited political impact since it offered Indians nominal administrative positions well away from the executive, did reveal one important fact. The ballot was dominated by Congress, while the All-India Muslim League returned a generally disappointing result. If the Muslim minority feared being overwhelmed at the ballot by the Hindu majority, then this proved that it would likely be so. It was now time for action.

In 1939, the Governor-General, without consultation, committed India to Imperial and Allied defense in World War II. This had the twin effect of pitching the recently empowered provisional authorities into rebellion, but also it galvanized the Muslim League to act. Muhammad Ali Jinnah, who was by then president of the League, persuaded participants at the 1940 annual congress of the party, held in Lahore, to adopt what later came to be known as the Lahore Resolution. This, in its simplest terms, demanded the division of India into two separate sovereign states — one Muslim, the other Hindu. This was the first definitive articulation of what later came to known as the Two Nation Theory. Although the notion of Pakistan as a separate state had been under discussion from as early as 1930, it had gained very little currency. However, a renewed antipathy between Hindus and Muslims in the aftermath of provincial elections breathed new life into the idea, and once it found expression at a national level, it more or less became de facto.

Congress, under the leadership of Jawaharlal Nehru, naturally rejected the principal of separate electorates outright, maintaining its claim of the only universal, authentic representative of all Indians. There were only two powers in India, Nehru claimed: Congress and the British government.

Planning the Partition

"We have undoubtedly achieved Pakistan, and that too without bloody war, practically peacefully, by moral and intellectual force, and with the power of the pen, which is no less mighty than that of the sword and so our righteous cause has triumphed." - Jinnah

In 1933, Muslim nationalist Choudhry Rahmat Ali created the hybrid name "Pakistan", further drawing a circle around the northern provinces of India. The name was created by taking "P" from Punjab, "A" from Afghanistan (which was then the North West Frontier Province), "K" from Kashmir, "S" from Sind and "tan" from Baluchistan — no clearer articulation that this was required to illustrate the scope of the future autonomous Muslim territory.

To a large extent, the widening gap between the two Indian nationalist parties was the product of the difference in personalities between Gandhi, Nehru, and Jinnah. Gandhi resigned from Congress in 1934, for reasons he explained as an unwillingness to be associated with certain Congress policies and for what he saw as indiscipline in the ranks of the party. Others have suggested that his eccentric style of politics and activism was simply no longer compatible with a party preparing practical strategies for an exchange of power. It is also perhaps true that Gandhi's growing popularity and charisma competed uncomfortably with the public profiles of more than one influential leader of Congress. One such was Jawaharlal Nehru, who was perhaps closest to the British insofar as his father was a Privy Counsellor, and he himself was very much a product of the British establishment. His father had conditioned him for rule, and he was certainly first in line for the Indian nationalist throne.

In this regard, Indian partition has increasingly in recent years been portrayed as a dual between two individuals fixated on personal power. Gandhi had no interest in power, and so the other individual was Jinnah. Due to his actions as a spoiler, he is often cast as the villain. Jinnah certainly did take an enigmatic position, championing first Indian unity and then distorting that position increasingly to a point when he would consider or hear nothing but partition. Jinnah would achieve partition, but he would never gain the same political heights enjoyed by Nehru and would, perhaps justly, carry the burden of blame for the disaster that followed.

The journey toward the goal of partition continued on March 23, 1940, with the Muslim League announcement of the Lahore Resolution, known also as the Pakistan Resolution. This would prove to be the final, definitive statement of Muslim League intention to pursue the two-state solution. A day before the resolution was published, Jinnah delivered a detailed address to an assembled audience of Muslim League members, clear in its implications and which stated in part, "Musalmans are a nation according to any definition of a nation, and they must have their homeland, their territory and their state."

Jinnah then went on to add, "It is extremely difficult to appreciate why our Hindu friends fail to understand the real nature of Islam and Hinduism. They are not religions in the strict sense of the word, but are, in fact, different and distinct social orders; and it is a dream that the Hindus and Muslims can ever evolve a common nationality; and this misconception of one Indian nation has gone far beyond the limits and is the cause of more of our troubles and will lead India to destruction if we fail to revise our notions in time. The Hindus and Muslims belong to two different religious philosophies, social customs, and literature[s]. They neither intermarry nor interdine together, and indeed they belong to two different civilizations which are based mainly on conflicting ideas and conceptions. Their aspects [perspectives] on life, and of life, are different. It is quite clear that Hindus and Mussalmans derive their inspiration from different sources of history. They have different epics, their heroes are different, and different episode[s]. Very often the hero of one is a foe of the other, and likewise their victories and defeats overlap. To yoke together two such nations under a single state, one as a numerical minority and the other as a majority, must lead to growing discontent, and final. destruction of any fabric that may be so built up for the government of such a state."

Thereafter, the matter of the two-state solution assumed less the aspect of a suggestion than a negotiation. Now that the concept was embedded in the popular consciousness, the question simply became one of establishing practical steps toward it. On July 1, 1940, Jinnah presented a series of proposals to the British government, known as the "Tentative Proposals of Jinnah". These were indeed tentative and said very little about anything, other than perhaps that no successful constitutional strategy for disengagement would be possible without Muslim consent, and Muslim consent would be granted to no solution that fell short of two nations.

Naturally, Britain was entirely consumed by the war effort in 1940, especially the necessity of defending the British Isles from direct German invasion in what has since come to known as the Battle of Britain. Metropolitan Britain was in no position to deal with difficult issues in India, and in practical terms, all other matters were subordinated to the British fight for survival. Once again, however, India would provide a vital bulwark against a German victory in this war, in particular since the Axis powers included Japan this time. The Japanese invasion of Burma, completed in 1942, brought the war to the very borders of India, and Indian compliance in imperial defense was never more vital than now.

It was then that Congress announced its "Quit India" campaign, essentially trading Indian cooperation in the war effort for a firm promise of independence upon an Allied victory. This was a risky move; after all, an Allied defeat would have meant an Axis Victory, which for India would have meant trading Britain as an imperial power for Japan. That would certainly crown Congress's "Quit India" campaign with success, but it might prove to be a pyrrhic victory. The British, however, were in no mood to spar with an opportunistic Congress leadership and clapped the entire top strata in irons, including Gandhi, incarcerating them for the remainder of the war. Congress, therefore, was largely inactive during this period, leaving Jinnah and the Muslim League an open field to cultivate their friendly relations with Britain. It was a poke in the eye for Congress, and Jinnah made the most of it.

Perhaps inevitably, these moves did not silence Indian dissent. Other factors were at play that would prove pivotal in India's journey to independence. Britain was reeling under German attacks, and pleas by Churchill for the United States to enter the war were met by a series of conditions that served to define the terms of the New World Order. One such was the Atlantic Charter, a cornerstone of the United States' view of a changing world. The Atlantic Charter defined Allied post-war objectives, among which were the principles of self-determination, sovereignty, and independence. The British had no choice but to comply with this. The British no longer led the world, and the United States was in favor of Indian independence.

Thus, in March 1942, a senior British cabinet minister (Member of Parliament, Minister of Aircraft Production, and Leader of the House of Commons), Sir Stafford Cripps, arrived in India on a mission to mollify dissent, douse fires among the ranks of Congress, and set the tone for the post-war solution. Trust, however, was entirely absent, and while Cripps offered a virtual blank check on independence at the end of the war, Gandhi, for one, was apt to remark that it was a check drawn on a collapsing bank.

Cripps

Nonetheless, Indian loyalty held during the war, and as Indian manpower mobilized after victory in Europe to drive the Japanese out of Burma, what Cripps had promised appeared in the end to be a self-fulfilling strategy. Winston Churchill won the war, but he did not survive the peace, and the Conservative Party was defeated in the general election of 1945 and replaced by the Labor government of Prime Minister Clement Attlee. Attlee was pro-Indian independence, and almost as soon as he took office, the formal process began.

The Viceroy of India, General Lord Archibald Wavell, was a military man of the North African and South Asian theatres who had little patience with political posturing. He recognized that the

British were finished in India, and so the sooner a British departure could be negotiated, the better. He was also a pragmatist and was prepared to cut through the political bunkum and see the situation for what it was. Congress wished to control a united India, claiming to speak for all Indians, while the Muslim League wished to achieve a two-state solution, ostensibly to protect the religious and cultural exclusivity of Indian Muslims. Behind that was Nehru, poised to assume power, and Jinnah, who wished to lead a nation and not merely a Muslim majority province of a country that Nehru ruled.

Wavell

On September 19, 1945, therefore, Wavell announced that elections to the provincial and central legislatures would be held between December 1945 and January 1946. From the results of this, an executive council would be formed and a constitution-making body convened to take the process forward. This was the first unequivocal British move toward a phased handover of power. In preparation, the British began releasing the leadership of Congress from prison, including Nehru.

The results of the election surprised no one. Congress won more or less every Hindu seat and the Muslim League won every Muslim seat. A few seats here and there went to such parties as the Indian Communist Party, but the overall message was perfectly clear.

In March, following this up, Attlee dispatched a cabinet mission to India to begin negotiating the practical terms of a British handover of power. The mission was headed by Lord Pethick-Lawrence, the Secretary of State for India, Cripps, and A. V. Alexander, the First Lord of the Admiralty. Wavell was present throughout, but he did not participate in negotiations. This was arguably one of the most important British diplomatic missions of the century. It was mounted on the understanding that Indian independence was inevitable and, moreover, that the terms of devolution and the success of the process as a whole would set the tone for what would inevitably be a wider process of decolonization across the former British Empire.

Ideally, the British hoped to retain India within the system of its own defense, even after granting its independence, and thus the British Commonwealth was offered as a future vehicle of common interest. However, the immediate objective was not to be prepared for future wars but to attempt to frame a constitution and establish a constitutional committee and thereafter set up a functioning executive council with bipartisan support from both major parties. At the root of negotiations was the need to establish some sort of power-sharing formula acceptable to both sides. There was about this phase of the mission a certain weary formality, and one can imagine that the likes of Cripps went through the motions in the full and certain knowledge that no such unified India was possible. Muslim fears that the British Raj would simply evolve into the Hindu Raj were not unfounded, and Congress certainly pressed its claim to speak on behalf of all Indians with tangible determination. Gandhi preached unity, but he had little of practical value to offer at that moment, and with matters now transcending the pulpit, Gandhi, in many respects, had become something of a liability.

On May 16, 1946, after initial dialogue with each side, the cabinet mission released its preliminary proposals for the composition of the new government. In these proposals, the creation of a separate Muslim Pakistan was ruled out, but at the same time, a wide enough crack was left in the door for a more general interpretation to be possible. What was proposed was a complicated federal system whereby a central government would be responsible for national affairs — foreign affairs, defense, transport, and communication — while a three-tier system of regional blocs would reserve wide powers for domestic administration. This would provide for independence as a British overseas dominion, fully engaged in the Commonwealth and remaining firmly within the British sphere of influence. It was a loosely configured concept that was all things to all people, and the prerequisite was simply that Indian politicians ratify it by accepting office as responsible ministers in the proposed government.

Jinnah and the Muslim league were quick to accept the plan, but Congress rejected it outright. Nehru held a press conference in Bombay declaring that Congress had agreed only to participate in the Constituent Assembly and regarded itself free to change or modify the Cabinet Mission Plan as it thought best. This prompted an immediate Muslim League walk out, which, no doubt, was the intention.

And so it went. Cripps might have felt that he had seen all of this before, and although British officials were formally required to discourage discussion of two states, it is unlikely that any of them saw any real alternative. This was confirmed at the end of July 1946 when Jinnah held a press conference at his Bombay home, where he declared once again his intention of creating Pakistan, intimating very generally that, if necessary, a violent struggle would be the means by which this would be achieved. When asked to specify, Jinnah responded with the comment, "Go to the Congress and ask them their plans. When they take you into their confidence I will take you into mine. Why do you expect me alone to sit with folded hands? I also am going to make trouble." The next day, he announced that August 16, 1946 would be "Direct Action Day". What this meant was left vague, but it was understood that meetings would be held here and there and no more than commonplace levels of disturbance encouraged simply to make a point. In general, this is what happened, but in one particular instance, in a sign of things to come, matters escalated beyond anything anyone could have foreseen.

The minutia of what led to the events in Calcutta on that day has been widely studied and debated, but what is clear is that communal violence on an unprecedented scale broke out. The general view of the matter is that violence was provoked first by Muslim demonstrators, but soon it became general, with a death toll estimated at between 7,000-10,000 Hindus, Muslims, and Sikhs. All sides considered their community the victims, and each blamed the other. The British authorities were charged with being slow to act, which is probably true. Preparations had certainly been inadequate, but no degree of preparation could really have prevented what took place. The violence continued for several days, sparking similar riots elsewhere, after which, for the next few months, clashes between the communities flared up periodically. In the aftermath, the British-brokered coalition government collapsed, and Jinnah announced an end to constitutional methods. "Today we have forged a pistol," he declared. "And [we] are in a position to use it."

Violence

"Any idea of a united India could never have worked and in my judgement would have led us to disaster." – Muhammad Ali Jinnah

August 1946 certainly was the turning point, and for the first time, elements within Congress itself began to air the possibility of a two-state solution. The British government retreated, recognizing that there was only so much that could be done and that ultimately the formula for independence lay in Indian hands. A deadline of no later than June 1948 was set for a transfer of power, which served clear notice on India to get its house in order. At more or less the same time, Prime Minister Attlee withdrew Lord Wavell as Governor General, replacing him with a more malleable personality in the form of Lord Louis Mountbatten, who was charged with overseeing the transition of power.

Mountbatten

Mountbatten, a fixture of the British aristocracy, was an odd, but perhaps inspired choice for this epoch-making appointment. Often criticized for his lack of intelligence, creativity, and leadership flair, he could well be regarded as a member of the very British class that thrived on Imperial India. He certainly enjoyed an august career and much imperial authority, based less on his ability than his birthright. To be appointed to this delicate diplomatic responsibility by a Labor prime minister was certainly unexpected, but perhaps the very Anglocentric nature of all three Indian nationalists in the picture, Gandhi included, demanded the involvement of such a British establishment figure. His instructions were simply to oversee the transition of power, get Britain out of India as cleanly and quickly as possible, and to avoid in the process any unnecessary damage to the reputation of Britain.

Matters were complicated a little by Mountbatten's personal friendship with Nehru, a fondness that was reciprocated by Nehru mainly in an untoward affection for Mountbatten's wife. Edwina Mountbatten, a powerful force in her own right, is rumored to have been intimate with Nehru and counted herself among the many European women who resided within the exclusive inner circle of the Mahatma. This comfortable union of the viceregal family and the Congress hierarchy had the effect of alienating Jinnah, who was always very chilly towards Mountbatten. Likewise, Mountbatten found the nervous, chain-smoking, and austere Jinnah a man entirely outside of his scope of understanding. His dealings with him, therefore, were stiff and reserved and without the easy familiarity that he enjoyed with Nehru and Gandhi.

In his first meeting with Jinnah on April 5, 1947, Mountbatten attended to the formality of persuading the Muslim leader to accept independence within a united India, but he was not in the least disturbed or surprised when this was rejected immediately. Thereafter, Mountbatten set to work preparing India for independence under the principle of partition. He brought forward the deadline six months, establishing August 15, 1947 as the provisional date of independence. This gave a total of four months for the complicated separation to be achieved. Congress by then had come to accept this inevitability, and only Gandhi, his power base now largely symbolic, continued to urge Mountbatten to persevere in searching for a formula for a united India. As an indication, some were apt to observe, of Gandhi's growing estrangement from reality, he urged Mountbatten to invite Jinnah to form a new central government, which Mountbatten wisely chose not to propose nor discuss with Gandhi's colleagues in the nationalist movement.

The first issue that Mountbatten was required to deal with was the question of the Princely States, and it is perhaps thanks to his own aristocratic origins that he was able to both sympathize with the erosion of hereditary rule but at the same time persuade the princes that their only course of action was to ally with one of the democratic nations in incubation. There were those kingdoms that would not, of course (namely Hyderabad, Jammu and Kashmir, and Junagadh), which sadly sowed the seeds of much future tension between India and Pakistan.

On June 3, 1947, Mountbatten presented his plan, refreshingly simple in the context of so much political complexity. The main points of the plans presented the likelihood of a sub-partition of Punjab and Bengal between the two states, but leaving the ultimate decision in the hands of the respective legislative assemblies of each province. The same was true for the northern provinces of Sind and Baluchistan, while a referendum would be held to determine the direction of the North West Frontier Province and the Sylhet district of Assam. No separate independence would be considered for the province of Bengal, and the future borders of the two states would be decided by a boundary commission.

Criticism was heaped on the plan from all sides for all kinds of reasons, but with the blunt determination of a sterile-minded man, Mountbatten simply closed the book on the matter and moved on to the next question. Congress accepted the proposals, recognizing perhaps, as the deadline approached, that the moment was not opportune for political bickering. Thereafter, all sides watched with interest as the work of the boundary commission began. The boundary commission was chaired by Sir Cyril John Radcliffe, 1st Viscount, a British lawyer, and Law Lord, supported by two Indian judges. The unenviable task handed to Radcliffe was to devise a territorial formula that would leave as many Hindus and Sikhs in India and as many Muslims in Pakistan as possible. For this purpose, broad delineations could be made of Hindu-dominated or Muslim-dominated regions, but no amount of creative penmanship could achieve a complete separation of the communities. The new boundaries were strategically announced only on August 14, 1947, the very day of Pakistan's independence and a day before India became independent. They were, therefore, a *fait accompli*, and in his typical style, Mountbatten let it be known that both sides could like it or leave it.

Meanwhile, in an atmosphere of almost frantic haste, the British Parliament began to debate the Indian Independence Act, which was granted royal assent on July 18, 1947. Provisions for a British withdrawal and the division of British India into two fully sovereign dominions of India and Pakistan were ratified before the boundaries of the new states had even been established.

As a result, some 14 million individuals, Muslim and Hindu, were stranded on the wrong side of their respective borders, and as the countdown to independence began, a mass migration of Hindus from Pakistan to India and of Muslims from India to Pakistan began. What followed was one of the greatest bouts of attempted genocide and ethnic cleansing in all of human history.

The partition is typically portrayed by history as an act of shameful abandonment by the British, but from the point of view of the British, who watched the horror play out as they were drawing up the gangplank, they were damned if they did and damned if they did not. The "Quit India" movement had announced both the Indian demand and the Indian haste to be rid of the British, but when the British did depart and the limitations imposed by their secular authority were lifted, India descended into anarchic violence and bloodshed. This prompted even greater criticism to be leveled against the British for leaving.

Be that as it may, however, Attlee, Wavell, and Mountbatten, and no doubt many others too realized that the time had come and that there would be no easy way to get the job done. If Mountbatten had been charged with achieving a difficult separation with a minimum of damage to the British reputation, then he probably failed, but at the same time, there was no real formula for success. Indians were ready to settle scores, and if British rule was all that was keeping them apart, then they were more than anxious to see the British gone.

Indeed, as the curtain began to fall on British India, Indians fell upon one another, and a thousand years of simmering antipathy exploded in an orgy of communal violence. The focus of violence in the immediate independence period tended to be concentrated in the Punjab and Bengal, the two Indian provinces that had themselves been partitioned by the delineation of boundaries. Both were regions relatively evenly populated by Hindus and Muslims, and the vast demographic shift that partition set in motion triggered a bout of retributional violence that favored none and spared none.

In the Punjab, some 4.5 million Hindus and Sikhs abandoned the western regions of the province and flooded into the east, while a higher number of Muslims migrated in the opposite direction. The British authorities, responsible for maintaining peace and order, were hopelessly overwhelmed by the scale of the violence, and in the end they mounted an inadequate and under-resourced response. By the time some order had been returned to the province (and even this was extremely limited), anywhere between 180,000 and 500,000 Hindus, Sikhs, and Muslims had perished, often under circumstances of excruciating violence.

The situation in Bengal, already partitioned in 1905, was somewhat less incendiary, but it too formed one of the numerous epicentres of violence. Several provincial cities were also rocked by communal violence, with Delhi, Bombay, Karachi, and Quetta in particular bearing the brunt. The violence was indiscriminate both in its perpetrators and victims. Peasants, the middle-classes, blue and white collar workers, religious persons, men and women, Hindus and Muslims were all implicated. Muslims who were forcibly removed from majority Hindu areas of India, their business and properties seized, made their way to Pakistan and subsequently joined the frenzy of anti-Hindu violence. Within the communities, fingers were pointed and continue to be pointed, but neither side can reasonably claim a monopoly on the role of victim or deflect culpability. It was communal violence in the true sense of the word.

During the initial independence phase, the figure typically quoted for general displacement is some 14 million, although many claim this is conservative and does not take into account those affected by the violence who did not migrate. The death toll also ranges widely, from 200,000-2 million. Truth be told, any figure within that range could plausibly be considered as good as any other.

The violence and mass refugee migrations continued into 1948, reaching a crescendo with the assassination of Gandhi on January 30 of that year. Throughout the violence, Gandhi had maintained his universalist position, appealing for calm and reconciliation and conducting regular inter-faith prayer vigils in various affected areas. On the day of his assassination, he was in Delhi, and as he was preparing for such a meeting, he was shot three times. His killer, Nathuram Godse, was a member of the extremist Hindu militant group Hindu Mahasabh, and the stated reason for his actions was Gandhi's accommodation of Muslims and advocacy of tolerance. Godse accused Gandhi of subjectivism and of acting as if only he had a monopoly of the truth. Godse, who had planned the assassination with, among others, fellow Hindu extremist Narayan Apte, was tried and convicted of murder. Both men were executed in 1949. The upswell of violence that followed Gandhi's death involved an inter-Hindu conflict as well as an increase in communal violence. Nathuram Godse was a Chitpavan Brahmin, and heavy reprisals were wrought against that community by various Congress supporters, most notably in the western Maharashtra State.

Godse

Further massacres were recorded across northern India and southern Pakistan, with, in addition to Punjab and Bengal, significant dislocation affecting the Sindh province. Sindh, now a province of Pakistan, hosted a large Hindu and Sikh minority, and it saw a mass exodus of some 800,000 Hindus to India, mainly to Bombay and Maharashtra. The death toll in this episode is unknown, but it was at least in the tens of thousands and possibly hundreds of thousands. More localized bouts of violence were recorded in Delhi, Alwar and Bharatpur, and Jammu and Kashmir.

Beginning in 1948, an orchestrated program gathered momentum on both sides of the border to begin the process of resettlement, and the dust of the whole brutal affair only began to settle toward the end of the decade.

Indian Independence Day is marked on August 15, and every year on that day, India rolls out a spectacle of pomp and ceremony that reflects in every detail the curious love affair the country still enjoys with Britain. The accoutrements of empire still decorate Indian military traditions, and the residues of British India remain visible almost everywhere. On that day in 1947, however, as Lord Mountbatten stood in his viceregal uniform, a figure from another era, and handed over power to the simply attired Indian leadership, a new age began.

As the British Raj slipped away into history and as the sun began to set on the British Empire, small nations across the world were watching very closely. Six years later, another venerable bastion of the British imperial age fell to a military coup. Egypt entered the revolutionary field, inspired by the emerging Cold War and strategically positioned astride the Suez Canal. The Suez Crisis, the British military intervention, and the British military humiliation finally alerted the British to a new reality. Soon the Gold Coast was independent, and then Nigeria, Jamaica, Kenya, Uganda, and many others were free as the dominos began to fall.

Many of those transitions were violent and many followed a similar pattern, but India remained the test case. The Indian and Pakistani individual relationship with Britain survived, but their relationship with one another was never healed. Partition is usually remembered for the sake of its violence, and violence certainly did occur on an epic scale. "Holocaust" is a word now frequently used, and each side still consistently blames the other. However, the violence was only a part of the picture. The Muslim-Hindu divide pre-existed all modern political machinations, and partition was an equalization simply waiting to happen. India and Pakistan are artificial creations of an imperial power that did not take any of this into account. As was true in many other cases and many other colonies, when the time came, the British were all too keen to jump ship, and the British were slow to accept responsibility for the aftermath or what could have been done differently.

One such result is the cold war between India and Pakistan that has been simmering since the partition. The frontier between India and Pakistan remains one of the most potentially volatile in the world, and these two societies, which have uneasily coexisted alongside one another for centuries, remain today as immiscible as oil and water.

Online Resources

Other British history titles by Charles River Editors

Other titles about the Sepoy Rebellion on Amazon

Other titles about the British Raj on Amazon

Bibliography

Allan, J. T. Haig, Wolseley and H. H. Dodwell, *The Cambridge Shorter History of India*, ed. H. H. Dodwell. Cambridge, England: Cambridge University Press, 1934.

Allen, Charles. *Soldier Sahibs: The Daring Adventurers Who Tamed India's Northwest*

Frontier. New York: Carroll and Graf Publishers, 2000.

Barua, Pradeep P. *Gentlemen of the Raj: The Indian Army Officer Corps, 1817-1949.* Westport, CT: Praeger, 2003.

Bhatnagar, G. D. *Awadh under Wajid `Ali Shah*. Bharatiya Vidya Prakashan, Varanasi, 1968.

Carr, Robert. "Concession & Repression: British Rule in India 1857-1919: Robert Carr Assesses the Nature of British Rule in India during a Key, Transitional Phase," *History Review*, no. 52 (2005).

Cavendish, Richard. "The Black Hole of Calcutta." *History Today* Volume 56. Issue 6. June 2006.

Connerney, Richard. *The Upside-Down Tree: India's Changing Culture*. New York: Algora, 2009.

Cross, Colin. *The Liberals in Power, 1905-1914.* London: Barrie and Rockliff, 1963.

Dalrymple, William. *The Last Mughal: The Fall of a Dynasty: Delhi, 1857*. New York: Alfred A. Knopf, 2007.

Devsare, Harikrishna. *Mangal Pande*. Prabhat Prakashan, 2006.

"East India Company and Raj 1785-1858" About Parliament. www.parliament.uk

Derbyshire, I. D. "Economic Change and the Railways in North India, 1860-1914." *Modern Asian Studies* 21, no. 3 (1987): 522.

Dewey, Clive. *Anglo-Indian Attitudes: Mind of the Indian Civil Service*. London: The Hambledon Press, 1993.

Forrest, George W., ed., *The Indian Mutiny 1757-1758: Selections from the Letters, Dispatches, and Other State Papers Preserved in the Military Department of the Government of India. Volume III.* New Delhi: Asian Educational Services, 2000.

Forster, Richard. "Mangal Pandey: Drug-crazed Fanatic or Canny Revolutionary?" *The Columbia Undergraduate Journal of South Asian Studies.*

Francavilla, Domenico. "Interacting Legal Orders and Child Marriages in India." *American University Journal of Gender Social Policy and Law* 19, no. 2 (2011): 535-538.

Goldman, Robert. *Journal of the American Oriental Society* 87, no. 3 (1967): 340-43.

doi:10.2307/597747.

Griffiths, Percival. *The British Impact on India*. London: MacDonald, 1952.

Guha, Ramachandra. "Churchill and Gandhi", *The Hindu Magazine*. June 19, 2005.

Herbert, Christopher. *War of No Pity: The Indian Mutiny and Victorian Trauma*. Princeton: Princeton University Press, 2008.

Keay, John. *India: A History*. New York: Atlantic Monthly Press, 2000.

Keene, H.G. History of India: From the Earliest Times to the End of the Nineteenth Century, Vol. II. Edinburgh: John Grant, 1906.

"Meerut." The Cheltenham Looker-on. September 26, 1857.

Metcalf, Thomas R. *Ideologies of the Raj*, V.3, Part 4 New York: Cambridge University Press, 1995.

Mukherjee, Rudrangshu. *Awadh in Revolt, 1857-1858: A Study of Popular Resistance*. Delhi: Permanent Black, 2001.

"Mutiny in the Empire." The Telegraph. 31 August 1996.

New World Encyclopedia contributors, "Indian Rebellion of 1857," New World Encyclopedia, http://www.newworldencyclopedia.org/p/index.php?title=Indian_Rebellion_of_1857&oldid=9 80264 (accessed November 13, 2016).

Palmer, J.A.B. *The Mutiny Outbreak at Meerut in 1857.* Cambridge: Cambridge University Press.

Pati, Biswamoy. *The Great Rebellion of 1857 in India*. New York: Routledge, 2010.

Ram, Sita. *From Sepoy To Subedar: Being The Life and Adventures of Subedar Sita Ram A Native Officer of the Bengal Army, Written and Related by Himself.* Ed., James Lunt. Delhi: Vikas Publications, 1873.

Rotton, John Edward Wharton. *The Chaplain's Narrative of the Siege of Delhi*. London: Smith, Elder, and Company, 1858.

"The Sepoy Rebellion". *The London Quarterly Review*. No. XVII, October 1857, ii.

Shadle, Robert et al., eds., *Historical Dictionary of European Imperialism*. New York:

Discounted Books by Charles River Editors

We have titles at a discount price of just 99 cents everyday. To see which of our titles are currently 99 cents, click on this link.

Made in the USA
San Bernardino, CA
29 December 2019

62476385R00062